Foundation Themes

The Seaside

Victoria Farrow

Text © 2004 Victoria Farrow
© 2004 Scholastic Ltd

Designed using Adobe InDesign

Published by Scholastic Ltd
Villiers House
Clarendon Avenue
Leamington Spa
Warwickshire CV32 5PR

Visit our website at www.scholastic.co.uk

Printed by Belmont Press

1 2 3 4 5 6 7 8 9 0   4 5 6 7 8 9 0 1 2 3

Author
Victoria Farrow

Editor
Susan Howard

Assistant Editor
Victoria Lee

Series Designer
Joy Monkhouse

Designer
Andrea Lewis

Illustrations
Louise Gardner

Cover photography
©Digital Vision Ltd

Acknowledgements

The publishers gratefully acknowledge permission to reproduce the following copyright material:

Qualifications and Curriculum Authority for the use of extracts from the QCA/DfEE document *Curriculum Guidance for the Foundation Stage* © 2000 Qualifications and Curriculum Authority

Sanchia Sewell for the use of 'Grab your hat', 'My bucket is full', 'Your footprints', 'Here are some boats', 'Swimming fish' and 'On a sunny day' © 2004, Sanchia Sewell, all previously unpublished.

Brenda Williams for the use of 'Sitting in the sand at the seaside', 'Donkey rides', 'How many fishes?', 'Five coloured boats', 'A mermaid sings' and 'I'm going to the seaside!' © 2004, Brenda Williams, all previously unpublished.

Every effort has been made to trace copyright holders and the publishers apologise for any inadvertent omissions.

British Library Cataloguing-in-Publication Data A catalogue record for this book is available from the British Library.

ISBN 0 439 97119 5

Contents

Chapter 1

At the seaside

Chapter 3

Seaside games

Chapter 2

On the beach

Chapter 4

On the sea

Contents

Foundation Themes
The Seaside

Introduction

Personal, social and emotional development

Communication, language and literacy

Mathematical development

Knowledge and understanding of the world

Physical development

Creative development

This book is one of the titles in the *Foundation Themes* series of books that provide activities all based on one complete theme, packed with original activities suitable for everyone working with children in the Foundation Stage. Each book focuses on a popular theme and provides step-by-step activities with Stepping Stone and Early Learning Goal clearly indicated.

The activities are aimed at all settings working with three- to five-year-old children, including nursery and Reception classes, playgroups and day nurseries. The activities cover the six Areas of Learning and include support and extension ideas to help provide for younger children needing extra support or older children requiring extension in their learning. The books include photocopiable resources designed to support individual activities, newly-commissioned songs and rhymes to accompany the theme, ideas for circle-time sessions and new display ideas.

Using this book

A theme-based structure is widely used in most settings delivering an early years curriculum. It works particularly well in early years education, where one Area of Learning overlaps into another, linking all six Areas together through a common theme. You can begin your long-term planning by selecting themes for the year and drawing up topic webs that link all six Areas together.

The chapters in this book provide activities (one per page) linked to the six Areas of Learning as outlined in the QCA document, *Curriculum Guidance for the Foundation Stage*. Each activity is linked to a specific Stepping Stone, colour coded to show whether the activity is at the simplest level (yellow), at a higher level (blue) or at the highest level (green), to match the colours used to show progression in the QCA document. The Areas of Learning covered for each activity are identified by the logos shown in the panel (left).

Planning made easy

To save planning time all the activities, display ideas, songs and rhymes you will need to deliver a whole theme are provided here. The activities cover all six Areas of Learning, link in with your chosen theme and have appropriate learning objectives. A cross-curricular planner (pages 10 and 11) shows how the activities in the book cover the Foundation Stage curriculum and Early Learning Goals. Each activity comes with a list of resources that will be needed and an explanation of the preparation that is required. This can be incorporated into a short-term planning sheet. Evaluation and assessment ideas are also provided, with suggestions on how to record individual children's progress.

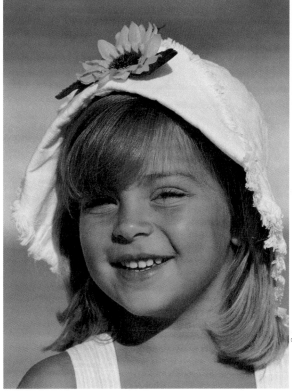

Foundation **Themes**
The Seaside

The seaside

'The seaside' is a popular and wide-reaching theme that can be approached from many different aspects. Sand and water, so popular with children of all ages, are readily available and found in most early years settings. Children can benefit from the sheer tactile enjoyment and discover the properties of wet and dry sand through sieving, pouring, shaping and moulding. Treasure can be buried and discovered, caught in a sieve or weighed in a balance.

Set up a water tray and find out about floating, sinking and capacity; discover which materials and shapes make the best boats, or build a makeshift boat in the role-play area to tell stories from. Make a rocking boat from a paper plate or fill a treasure chest with paper crowns and pasta necklaces.

Pirates are a firm favourite with young children, and provide an excellent stimulus for role-play and storytelling, singing and music-making. Maps, hats and telescopes can be made from paper and provide excellent props.

There are all sorts of weird and wonderful sea creatures to find out about, from sharks to jellyfish as well as everyday rock-pool creatures, limpets, sea anemones and crabs. Children can try to make their own models of sea creatures from paper plates, make clay prints to show the beautiful patterns of the scales on a fish and make wax-crayon rubbings of different sea shells.

Imagine and re-create the sounds of the seaside, identify footprints in the sand and join together on an imaginary journey to the beach. Set up a seaside café and choose a dish from the menu or enjoy a parcel of take-away fish and chips. Make a mermaid display and use the circle-time ideas to describe seaside treasures or imagine what it would be like to live as a mermaid in an undersea world.

© Victoria Farrow

Enjoying our world

All 60 of the activities in this book have been tried and tested with children in the three- to five-year-old age range. The children involved worked on 'The Seaside' theme for five weeks, finishing with a trip to the beach and local aquarium, where they found that the work done in their setting added greatly to their enjoyment of the day out. They had a greater understanding and appreciation for the wildlife and the seaside environment as well as a wealth of ideas for activities to enjoy once there.

Whether you live near the coast or in the middle of a city, the seaside is a fascinating and beautiful part of our children's environment. It is important for them to learn to appreciate and care for it. Hopefully most children will get the opportunity to visit the seaside at some point in their lives.

The ideas in this book are intended to be flexible and although it is appreciated that most settings have to spend the greater part of their day indoors, activities are provided that can be used in an outdoor play area or, with any luck, on the beach. It is still important for children to learn about the seaside environment even if they do not have the opportunity to witness it first-hand. By using the activities in this book together with some carefully chosen resources and a sprinkling of imagination, you can help to bring the seaside to life for every child.

Planning

I n this chapter, we take a look at the importance of thorough planning, and provide practical guidance on ways that you can work with staff and parents to ensure that all of the children in your setting benefit from high-quality learning opportunities.

The learning environment

Providing an environment that is stimulating, purposeful, challenging and supportive will give children beginning their education the best chance of developing into confident and successful learners.

Effective practice is based upon a well-planned programme, which reflects an understanding of how young children learn. It is important to establish clear aims for learning and to share these aims with all of the staff in your setting. Parents also play a vital role in their children's education, and you need to ensure that you and your team are working with them to promote their children's learning.

It is important to create a balance of adult-directed and child-directed activity with opportunities for small and large group learning as well as individual play. Sensitive and timely intervention by adults can reinforce and extend children's learning. The content should be balanced and promote the social, emotional, physical, intellectual and spiritual development of the individual child.

Children benefit from an environment that is safe, secure and fun to be in. They will flourish in a setting where they feel relaxed, confident and excited to learn. The activities that you plan should have a clear purpose, and it is important that they are stimulating as well as having clear learning objectives.

Written plans

Written plans provide a record that you can share and use for future reference. However, it is the planning process that is important and practitioners who meet regularly to discuss their plans and ideas may find that a simple format is sufficient for their written plans. Any written daily plan that you produce needs to be clear and concise, so that it can be easily interpreted and shared.

By using focused assessment targets and record-keeping based on direct observation and discussion, your future planning will be more relevant, building on children's previous experience and learning.

© Soda

The planning process
There are three stages to planning a programme of learning:

Long-term planning
This provides a framework for the Areas of Learning and Early Learning Goals and usually covers a year or, with a rolling programme, two years. It provides an overview of the range of learning opportunities that will be offered in your setting. It outlines which themes you plan to cover and when. It is a guide and should not be stuck to too rigidly. It is important to make the most of exciting unplanned events that capture the children's interest.

© Soda

Medium-term planning
This shows what will be covered during a term or half-term. It develops the long-term plans that you have made, providing more detail and considering the learning styles of the children in your group. Your medium-term plans should focus on particular aspects of learning, suggesting resources to be used and considering the best ways of achieving the learning intentions, and should take into account the number of children and adults in your group. This is also the stage at which you should decide upon the assessment methods that you will be using.

Short-term planning
Your short-term plans will bring the long- and medium-term plans forward to more detailed weekly and daily plans. At this stage, you can organise individual sessions and consider individual children's needs. You can make detailed decisions about the learning objectives and Early Learning Goals that you would like to focus on from week to week. Your short-term plans will outline the activities that you intend to carry out, the methods of teaching that you will use and the resources that you will need. You can also identify the role of each adult in your setting at this stage, and provide observation or record sheets where necessary.

Using themes
Once you have chosen your themes and fitted them in to your long-term plan, look at the time available during each half-term and choose a range of activities from the theme that cover the six Areas of Learning. Well ahead of time, read through the activities and start collecting and making teaching materials, so that all the resources are ready for the activities that you plan to do.

The activities provided in this book cover all six Areas of Learning and a wide range of Stepping Stones and Early Learning Goals. At the start of an activity identify the learning you wish to be gained, so that the objective of the activity is clear to everyone involved in the learning process. It is important that both adults and children are in no doubt as to what they are aiming to achieve. If, for example, the activity involves cutting, it is important to emphasise whether the object of the activity is to learn to control the scissors effectively or to produce a pleasing end result. This makes a big difference to the adults working with the children and to the way that the children tackle the activity.

When planning a programme of learning it is important to consider what children already know and can do. There are times when planned activities should give way to unplanned, yet valuable, spontaneous play. The children should be given opportunities to make choices in their learning and decisions in their play.

Many settings, in schools with a nursery and Reception class, for example, use a two-year rolling programme and choose topics that are relevant to the children's interests and local environment. Themes can be arranged to fit in to the school terms and topics selected that are appropriate to the seasons. It is also important to consider fixed dates in the school calendar and make sure that you keep the larger topics for parts of the year where there is more time available. Festivals, concerts, sports days and the like can involve a lot of practice and rehearsal time as can paper work and parent meetings. All these things should be taken into consideration when setting out your long-term plan.

Planning for the Foundation Stage

The Foundation Stage covers the period from age three to the end of Reception year. The Stepping Stones are the developmental targets for children from the age of three and lead on to the Early Learning Goals, which set out the expected attainment by most children by the end of the Foundation Stage.

The Learning objectives, Stepping Stones and Early Learning Goals, depending on the stage of development of each child, are outlined in the new Foundation Stage Profiles, which you will need to complete as part of your assessment process. When grouping children for activities that are to be assessed, it is important that you consider whether they should be grouped according to their stage of development or their age.

© Soda

Equal opportunities

Both girls and boys should be encouraged to take part in all of the activities on offer in your setting. Some children and adults have preconceived ideas about what girls and boys do, such as playing with cars or dolls. Children should be encouraged to experience a range of activities and to become skilled in a variety of areas. This may need sensitive adult intervention, ensuring that construction toys or cars do not become 'boy's toys' and dolls and soft toys are included in a variety of activities from an early stage.

Children who speak a second language will benefit by being able to discuss their ideas in both languages. If possible, ask an adult who speaks the child's home language to work alongside, enabling the child to develop the concepts that are being taught more fully.

Foundation Themes
The Seaside

Personal, social and emotional development

ELG clusters	Activity	Page
Dispositions and attitudes	Sailing-boats Follow the footprints Row, row, row your boat Floating jellyfish	18 43 54 68
Self-confidence and self-esteem	Ollie the octopus The mermaid's world	64 75
Making relationships	Swim, little fishy	40
Behaviour and self-control	Picnic time My mermaid friend	21 61
Sense of community	Safety at sea	77

Creative development

ELG clusters	Activity	Page
Exploring media and materials	Sandy souvenirs Beach collages Create a sea creature	33 36 63
Music	Songs of the sea	74
Imagination	Hats, maps and telescopes Seaside dance	51 73
Responding to experiences, and expressing and communicating ideas	Sounds of the sea She sells sea shells Fishy prints	26 28 60

Foundation Themes

Physical development

ELG clusters	Activity	Page
Movement	Sharks! Catch the fish Treasure trail Making waves	41 42 48 58
Sense of space	Sand sculptures	34
Health and bodily awareness	Fish and chips! Seaside music	17 25
Using equipment	Build a boat One by one	55 47
Using tools and materials	Rocking boats	53

Communication, language and literacy

The Seaside

 ## Mathematical development

 ## Knowledge and understanding of the world

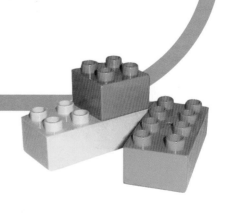

Children with special needs

Children with special educational needs will benefit from a well-planned curriculum and supportive adults. You will need to provide equal opportunities for children to join in fully in all of your group's activities regardless of their race, gender, culture, religion, social circumstances, ability or special educational needs. It is important to ensure that your setting has provision for children with specific physical needs, such as poorly developed motor control or impaired sight. The sandpaper letters and finger-painting activities in this book will help children to learn through touch. You should also aim to provide extra adult support to help prevent frustration with a child who cannot manipulate scissors or small objects.

Collecting resources

When building up a bank of resources it is well worth making your own materials and storing them carefully for future use. It is a good idea to laminate card resources for durability and store them in labelled plastic zip wallets. If you use a rolling programme and repeat themes perhaps every two years, it is essential that you keep everything labelled and properly stored, so that you can re-use your resources. A lot of materials can be adapted and used for other themes, so it is important to know where everything is. Large transparent project folders that can be hung up or laid flat are ideal for storing posters and zip wallets.

The majority of resources that are required for the activities in this book should be readily available in most early years settings.

Safety

Young children need constant supervision to ensure their safety and well-being. Sand and water will get spilled and children should be encouraged to help clean up that area as soon as this happens or to ask for assistance. To help prevent accidents, it is important that children are kept within view at all times, and are reminded frequently of safety issues, such as not putting toys in their mouths, not throwing the sand or sucking pens.

Home partnership

Parents can play an important part in the learning process by extending the work that you have been doing in your setting in their own homes through games and other activities. This reinforces learning and provides a link between home and your setting. Set aside time to talk to parents about this, explaining that learning should be fun and is most effective when practical. It should be a positive experience for both parents and children and not a chore. Explain that children should be encouraged to talk about what they are doing as they play, to ask and answer questions and solve problems. Parents will enjoy helping their children more when they realise how important it is to play games with them at this stage in their development.

© Soda

Assessment

I n this chapter, we take a look at effective strategies that you can use to observe and record the achievements of all of the children in your group, and show how these fit into the new Foundation Stage Profile.

Assessment is vital in order to help you plan for the next step in children's learning. Keeping track of what children have learned and understand means that you can plan the next activity by building on what they already know.

You can use observation sheets to make notes on particular children as they play, observing who the children interact with, how long they focus on a particular activity, which activities they choose and which they avoid. You can then discuss your observations with other staff members and make plans to target any areas of weakness.

© Derek Cooknell

Focused attainment targets

Focused attainment target sheets can be used when looking at a particular learning objective. Use a simple colour-coded system: green to show that the child achieved the target, orange if they were almost there and red if they did not achieve the target. By using this system it is easy to see at a glance which children need more time on a particular area of development and which are ready to move on. As well as colour-coding, you can also make more detailed notes when working with a small group of children, especially if they show a high or low level of understanding. It is just as important to stimulate the high achievers, as it is to support children who underachieve. Activities that are suitable for their stage of development will ensure a higher chance of success and enjoyment. The activities in this book all include a section on 'Support and extension'. This section provides suggestions for simplifying and extending the activity, to cater for children at different stages of development within your group.

Continual assessment

It is important to build up your assessment of each child over time and not assume that assessing a single activity is sufficient evidence to show whether a child did or did not achieve a particular goal. Children will perform differently on different days and at different times, depending on a variety of factors, and it is wise to build up a picture of each child's achievements before making conclusions.

Foundation Themes
The Seaside

In order to make an accurate assessment in any of the six Areas of Learning it is prudent to check each Early Learning Goal or Stepping Stone several times, on different days, with different activities and, if possible, with different adults involved in the assessing process. This will give you a clearer all-round picture of the child's development. Children can be tired, hungry, anxious or distracted for a number of reasons, all of which can affect their performance when being assessed. Assessments are not tests and children should not feel under pressure to perform a task in a certain way. Where you feel unsure about your judgement of a child, continue with assessment and observations in a variety of contexts within your setting. Encouraging young children to talk about what they are doing is an excellent way of assessing their understanding and for the adult involved to assess the child's level of comprehension as well as evaluating the activity. It is important to note whether each individual fully understood the concepts being taught or whether that child needs to redo the activity, go back a step or just be allowed more time to play freely with the activity and reinforce the learning process.

© Derek Cooknell

The Foundation Stage Profile

Your assessments should be built up over the year on a cumulative basis, from ongoing learning and teaching. By tracking a child's progress in an informal manner periodically throughout the year and recording it, it is possible to have a clear record of each child's rate of development in each Area. The Foundation Stage Profile booklets are designed for just this purpose, with a system of recording whether stages of development were reached during the autumn, spring or summer term.

As well as highlighting achievements it is useful to write comments about the child's progress, making the record system more personal and less formal. Relevant remarks about an activity a child particularly enjoyed and a record of comments made by the child during the activity make the whole assessment process seem more personal. The booklet then becomes a record of a well-understood individual child rather than an impersonal record of highlighted achievements. When new starters join your setting, talk to parents about their children in order to help you build up a picture of each individual child. Involve parents in discussions on a regular basis to keep them informed about their child's progress and ensure that relevant information is shared.

The Foundation Stage Profile replaces the statutory Baseline Assessment on entry to primary school and has been produced to help record each child's achievements and to ensure that, for children who move between settings, information gathered by one setting can be easily passed on to the next. It summarises a young child's achievements and provides important information for parents and Year 1 teachers. It also acknowledges the child's strengths and clearly identifies any weaknesses that may need addressing.

Chapter 1

At the seaside

The activities in this chapter provide the perfect introduction to a theme on the seaside. Explore the sights and sounds of the beach as you make musical instruments to mimic the sounds of the sea, set up a café selling delicious seaside food and enjoy your own exciting boat race!

'S' is for 'seaside'

Group size
Up to eight children.

What you need
A copy of the photocopiable sheet 'Seaside shapes' on page 89; seaside items beginning with 's' (for example, spade, sun-hat, sun-glasses, seagull, starfish, suncream); a cloth bag.

Preparation
Put the seaside items inside the cloth bag. Copy the photocopiable sheet on to card and cut out the pictures to make individual cards.

What to do
Sit on the floor and invite the children to join you in a circle. Begin by asking whether anyone has ever been to the seaside. Talk about the things that you might see and hear. Now ask the children to imagine that they are all sitting on the sand at the seaside. Ask them to think of any seaside words. As they offer suggestions, point out those words that begin with an 's' sound.

Invite the children to watch as you pull out and name the seaside items from the bag in turn. Each time you pull out an object, emphasise the initial 's' sound. Set the objects out in the middle of the circle. Describe one of the items, and invite the children to tell you which object they think is being described.

Now ask if anyone can tell you what sound all of these items begin with. Pass around the picture/word cards from the photocopiable sheet, making sure each child has a card. Ask them to read out the word on their card and to say whether or not it begins with 's'. Can they think of anything else beginning with 's'?

Finish by telling the children a simple seaside story using the cards or seaside items as props. Invite the children to contribute their own ideas to the story.

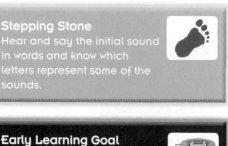

Stepping Stone
Hear and say the initial sound in words and know which letters represent some of the sounds.

Early Learning Goal
Link sounds to letters, naming and sounding the letters of the alphabet.

Support and extension
Younger children could try to identify the objects in the bag by feeling them. Give older children their own copy of the 'Seaside shapes' photocopiable sheet on page 89. Ask them to name each of the items beginning with 's', sound out the words and colour the pictures in. Invite them to have a go at writing some of the words.

Home partnership
Ask parents and carers to play games with their children at home, or on the journey home from your setting, searching for items beginning with 's'.

Further ideas
♦ Draw the letter 's' in wet sand using fingers, pencils and sand tools.
♦ Enjoy the rhyme 'Sitting in the sand at the seaside' on the photocopiable sheet on page 83.

Theme links
Nursery rhymes
Shapes

Foundation
Themes
The Seaside

Sights and sounds

Group size
Whole group.

What you need
The 'Seaside sounds' photocopiable sheet on page 90; clipboard; pencil; paper.

Preparation
Photocopy the 'Seaside sounds' sheet on to card and cut out the individual pictures to make nine cards. Attach the paper to the clipboard. Take the children on a short walk in and around your setting. Ask them to listen carefully to the different sounds that they can hear. Identify each one and draw a simple picture on the clipboard to represent the object that made each sound. When you have finished your walk, ask the children to help you to re-create each of the sounds.

What to do
Invite the children to close their eyes. Ask them to imagine that they are walking along a sandy beach. What sounds might they hear? Encourage the children to think about the animals and people that they might hear, as well as the sounds of the sea.

Show the children the picture cards. Talk about what is happening in each picture, and invite the children to help you to think of ways that you could make each of the sounds indicated in the pictures. As a group, try making each sound.

Now tell the children a story about a day at the seaside, incorporating each of the sounds that you have just made together. Tell the story a couple of times, encouraging everyone to join in with all of the sounds in the appropriate places. Now give each pair of children a picture card. Retell the story, this time inviting the pairs of children to make the sounds that are indicated on their card at the appropriate place in the story. Use the words 'loud' and 'quiet' for volume and 'quick' and 'slow' for the speed of the sound being made. For example: 'The donkey brayed quietly and slowly as he carried the children along the sand. Then he saw another donkey coming towards him carrying more happy children, and he brayed louder and faster'. Enjoy making up different versions of your seaside story, letting the children contribute their own ideas for the story line.

Support and extension
For younger children leave out the picture cards to begin with and make all the sounds together as a group. Older children could help younger children by sitting next to them and working in pairs.

Home partnership
Provide a sheet of picture sounds for children to listen out for on their journey to and from your setting. You could include noises such as a car, a plane, a bird, a baby crying, people talking and perhaps a siren.

Further ideas
♦ Use a tape recorder to record sounds around your setting. Have fun identifying each sound.
♦ Re-create the sounds using percussion instruments, or sand and water tools.
♦ Record your storytelling session for the children to listen to on other occasions.

Theme links
Opposites
Sounds

Foundation Themes
The Seaside

Fish and chips!

Group size
Up to four children.

What you need
Paper plates or trays; sponges; scissors; table; table-cloth; plastic vinegar and sauce bottles (make sure they are empty and clean); plastic knives and forks; newspaper; A4 card; felt-tipped pens.

Preparation
Cut out some fish and chip shapes from the sponges. Set up a table with a cloth, sauce bottles and plastic knives and forks. On A4 card, write a simple menu for a fish and chip shop, adding pictures next to each item.

What to do

Invite the children to think about times when they have been on holiday, or out on a day trip. What food did they eat? Did they have a picnic? Did anyone visit a restaurant? Tell the children that, at the seaside, many people like to buy fish and chips to eat. Has anyone ever had fish and chips at a restaurant? Maybe they have eaten chips out of a paper cone or some newspaper!

Show the children your seaside café. Explain that it sells delicious fish and chips. Can anyone suggest where the fish might have come from? Talk about fishing boats, and explain how the fish that we buy at the supermarket is caught by fishermen and brought ashore for us to enjoy. Look at the menu together. Talk about the different dishes on offer, inviting the children to talk about their likes and dislikes. Suggest other food and drinks that people enjoy at the seaside that you could add to the menu, such as hot dogs, ice-cream and cold drinks.

Show the children the sponge fish and chip shapes and invite them to take turns to be the waiter/waitress and customers in the café. Remind everyone to say, 'Please' and, 'Thank you', and reinforce the importance of washing hands before handling food or eating. Encourage the waiters and waitresses to ask the customers if they would like to eat in, or whether they would prefer to have their fish and chips wrapped in newspaper to take away!

When everyone has had a turn either buying or selling food in the café, gather the children together. Explain that, while chips might taste delicious, we should not eat them every day because they are not very healthy. Think of some healthy alternatives together, such as jacket potatoes. Discuss the importance of a healthy, varied diet. Can anyone tell you why sugary and fatty foods are not good for us? What other, healthier foods could we eat instead?

Support and extension

Provide pictures of food and drink that we might take on a seaside picnic. Include healthy and not so healthy items, such as milk, sugary drinks, fruit juice, crisps, apples, sweets and bread. Encourage younger children to work in pairs to sort the pictures into sets. Ask older children to explain how they have sorted the pictures.

Home partnership

Ask parents and carers to help their children to find healthy foods in the supermarket when they are out shopping. Encourage them to reinforce the messages about healthy and unhealthy foods at home.

Further ideas

◆ Set up an 'ice-cream parlour' or 'juice bar' and invent your own weird and wonderful menus together!
◆ Draw and paint posters to display in your seaside café to reinforce the importance of healthy eating and good hygiene.

Theme links
Food
Ourselves
People who help us

Sailing-boats

Group size
Up to six children.

What you need
Light blue, dark blue, grey, yellow, red and green sugar paper; plates; sheets of A4 card; PVA glue; spreaders; pencils; scissors, coloured card.

Preparation
Cut the light blue, dark blue and grey paper into squares, roughly 2cm x 2cm. Place each shade on a separate plate. Cut simple boat shapes and triangles to represent sails from the red and green paper, and circles from the yellow paper. Use the shapes to make a sample mosaic of a boat sailing on the sea, gluing the shapes to a sheet of A4 card.

What to do
Begin by talking to the children about the different things that we see on the water at the seaside.
We might see birds swimming, big ships carrying people or cargo, or perhaps little sailing-boats. Show the children your picture, and explain that this type of picture, which is made up of lots of little shapes, is called a mosaic. Invite the children to have a go at making their own seaside mosaic.

Show the children the squares of paper and the coloured boat and sail shapes. Give each child a sheet of A4 card. Encourage the children to draw a line across the centre of their card from left to right, and to cover the bottom section with PVA glue. Let them fill this bottom section with their own choice of blue or grey squares to represent the sea, leaving little spaces in between each square. Encourage the children to talk about the choices that they are making. Suggest using a different shade for the sky, to make it stand out from the sea. When the sky and sea are finished, invite the children to choose a boat shape and sails to add to their picture. Help with the assembly and positioning where necessary. Finally, add a bright yellow sun in the sky.

Mount each mosaic on coloured card and put them on display for everyone to admire.

Support and extension
Encourage younger children to discuss their work and to ask for help when they feel they need it. Provide additional colours for older children, and invite them to include additional features, such as a stormy sky or a colourful sunset.

Home partnership
Ask parents to try new activities with their children. Provide a photocopied sheet of ideas that they can do using equipment that they have at home, such as making seaside collages from natural materials, or making textured pictures using sand glued on to card.

Further idea
♦ Make collages using squares of fabrics with different textures. Ask the children to feel and describe the fabrics and say which ones they prefer and why.

Theme links
Colours
Patterns

Treasure chest

Stepping Stone
Use writing as a means of recording and communicating.
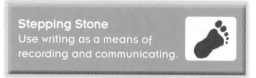

Early Learning Goal
Use their phonic knowledge to write simple regular words and make phonetically plausible attempts at more complex words.
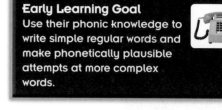

Group size
Any.

What you need
A4 white card; brown, yellow and orange paper; whiteboard; marker pen; glue.

Preparation
Cut out a large treasure chest shape from coloured paper and display it on the wall. Cut two pieces of A4 card into quarters. Make a word changer for each child by rolling a sheet of card into a tube and writing 'at' at one end. Slide a slightly wider tube, half the length of the first tube, on top with the letters 'c','m','h', 's','p','f','b' and 'r' written around the circumference (see illustration).

What to do
Ask the children to imagine that they are swimming deep under the ocean. Talk about the things that you might see, such as octopuses, sharks, shells and plants. Suggest that you might find a long-forgotten shipwreck, and prompt the children to suggest that there might be a treasure chest hidden on board! Draw the children's attention to the treasure chest shape on the wall. Can anyone think what treasure you might find inside it?

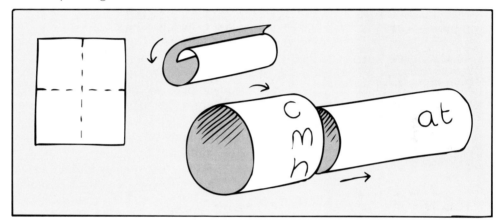

Explain that your treasure chest is going to be full of words. Invite the children to think of as many words as they can that end with 'at', such as 'cat' or 'bat'. Give each child a word changer. Demonstrate how to use the word changer, and ask the children to make the word 'cat'. See how many other words they can make. As they make new words, help them to write them down on the whiteboard. Copy the words on to the cards and then let the children stick them into the treasure chest to make a chest of words.

Invite the children to sit near the display and look at all the words in your treasure chest. Ask one of the children to point to a word, sound it out and make it on their word changer. Congratulate the children on their reading and writing skills and see if they can suggest any other words to add to the treasure chest.

Support and extension
Draw pictures next to the initial sounds on the word changer for younger children to help them read the words. For older children, make some word changers with different endings, such as 'ig' or 'en'.

Home partnership
Give parents and carers copies of the 'Words and pictures' photocopiable sheet on page 91. Ask them to use the cards to play games such as 'Lotto' and 'Snap', helping their children identify and sound out the letters in the words.

Further ideas
♦ Play rhyming catch. Say a simple consonant, vowel, consonant (CVC) word such as 'cat' and throw a beanbag to a child. The child should respond with a rhyming word and throw the beanbag back to you.
♦ Use the word changer to match two halves of a variety of seaside shapes, rather than letters. You could match two halves of a shell, a sand-castle, a boat, an ice-cream or a sun.

Theme links
Shapes
The alphabet

Fun at the fair

Group size
Up to ten children.

What you need
Plastic bottles; dry sand; funnels; spoons; sticky labels; pens; paper; beanbags; plastic pennies; pictures of seaside piers and fairgrounds; seaside music.

Preparation
Draw a numeral from 1 to 10 on each label.

What to do
Begin by showing the children a picture of a seaside pier or fairground. Ask them about their own experiences of fairgrounds. What kind of rides and games do they enjoy? Tell the children about a game called 'Skittles'. Has anyone ever played 'Skittles'? Invite them to share their experiences with the rest of the group, then ask the children if they would like to help you make a game of 'Skittles' that you can all enjoy.

Give each child a dry, empty plastic bottle and a sticky label. Ask them to look at the number on their label and to read it if they can. Encourage them to stick their label on to their bottle, then to pour in enough sand, using the funnels and spoons, to weigh the bottle down.

Decide on a price for your fairground game. Together, make a sign saying, for example, '2p a go'. Involve everyone in making tickets with the same wording. When you are ready to play, ask the children to listen carefully as they help you to set out the skittles. Arrange them in four rows: number 1 in the first row; 2 and 3 in the second row; 4, 5 and 6 in the third row and 7, 8, 9 and 10 in the back row. Encourage each child to wait until you say their number before placing their bottle in the correct position. Choose one child to be in charge of the tickets, then let the children take turns to buy a ticket for two pennies. Have fun trying to knock the skittles down with a beanbag, counting each time how many each child has knocked over.

Create a real fairground atmosphere by playing some appropriate music such as, 'We Do Like To Be Beside The Seaside'!

Support and extension
Help younger children to celebrate their success by cheering and clapping at their achievements. Encourage older children to praise each other and cheer their peers along.

Home partnership
Plan a simple funfair at your setting. Invite parents to help man the stalls and join in the fun with the children.

Further ideas
♦ Play other seaside games, such as digging for treasure in the sand tray with a spoon, throwing beanbags through hoops or magnetic fishing. Set up a refreshment stall, with ice lollies made from coloured card stuck on to lolly sticks, and tissue paper ice-cream in cardboard cones.
♦ Sing the song 'Grab your hat, your bucket and spade' on the photocopiable sheet on page 86.

Theme links
Number rhymes
Toys

Foundation Themes
The Seaside

Picnic time

Group size
Up to four children.

What you need
Two teddy bears or dolls; play food; plastic plates, cutlery and cups; picnic rug.

Preparation
Set up a beach scene with a picnic for two toys in the role-play area. Give one toy far more food than the other.

What to do
Talk to the children about the food that they might eat at the seaside. Ask whether anyone has ever been on a picnic. Where did they have their picnic? What food did they take with them? Explain that two lucky toys at your setting are having a picnic at the beach today.

Invite the children over to the role-play area to look at the toy's picnic. Does anyone notice anything odd? Perhaps one of the children might comment on the unfair distribution of food. If not, pretend that one of the toys wants to tell you something. Pick up the toy and ask what's wrong. Explain to the children that the toy thinks it is unfair that she has less food than her friend. Ask the children to suggest what could be done to remedy the situation. Consider their ideas and discuss ways of resolving the situation.

Invite one of the children to redistribute the food between the two toys so that it is, in their opinion, fair. Ask them if they think that the toys will be happy now. Do they think that the toy that has had food taken away from him will be happy? Discuss why it is important to think about others, to take turns and to share. Invite the children to talk about situations when they have been fair and shared their things with others.

Support and extension
With younger children, sit down at the picnic together and place the toys on your laps. Repeat the activity with the children more directly involved, and see if they find it easier to empathise with the toys. Older children may consider that some items of food are 'nicer' than others. If this is the case, discuss taking turns and choosing items of food as a fairer option.

Home partnership
Encourage parents and carers to play simple board games that encourage turn-taking and fairness, at home with their children.

Further ideas
♦ Make some seaside picnic food from play dough. Ask the children to share the food fairly. Discuss cutting cakes into pieces to share.
♦ Make some healthy seaside snacks and enjoy a picnic outside together. Try some fruity kebabs, cheese straws or salad sandwiches. Encourage the children to pass plates around, making sure that everyone has a fair share.

Theme links
Food
Number games

What's in my bucket?

Group size
Up to ten children.

What you need
Coloured card; drawing paper; crayons; glue sticks; plastic bucket; pictures of seaside items either drawn or cut from magazines.

Preparation
Fold the coloured card in half and cut a double bucket shape for each child, joined at the base so that it opens flat and you can look inside. Write a number from 1 to 10 on the front of each bucket.

What to do
Tell the children that, when you go to the seaside, you like to make sand-castles using your bucket and spade, and to collect things in your bucket. Show the children a real bucket and ask them to think of some things that they might find on a beach that they could put inside it. Their suggestions might include a crab or a shrimp from a rock pool, a limpet from a rock, a piece of seaweed that is lying on the sand, or perhaps a shell or pebble that they find near the edge of the water.

Give each child a card bucket. Ask them to look at the number on the front of their bucket to see how many things they need to put inside it. Provide pictures or let the children draw and cut out items to stick inside their buckets. Ask each child to count and check that they have the right number of items before closing their bucket and holding it by the handles. One at a time, invite the children to ask the rest of the group to guess how many items are inside their bucket. Can the child remember what they put inside their bucket?

Support and extension
For younger children, put dots inside their buckets to match the numbers on the front. Ask them to stick a picture on top of each dot then count them all. Older children could draw their own pictures and perhaps write a number by each one.

Home partnership
Encourage parents to play counting games with their children, for example, inviting them to put four shells or two plastic sea creatures in a bucket.

Further ideas
♦ Display the buckets in numerical order to make a bucket number line.
♦ Make the buckets in two contrasting colours and hang them up in a repeating pattern.

Theme links
Patterns
Sorting containers

Foundation Themes
The Seaside

Shell fans

Stepping Stone
Hear and say the initial sound in words and know which letters represent some of the sounds.

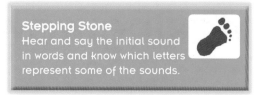

Early Learning Goal
Hear and say initial and final sounds in words, and short vowel sounds within words.

Group size
Up to ten children.

What you need
Oval-shaped pieces of white card, approximately 10cm long; split-pin fasteners; A4 white card; pen.

Preparation
Write individual letters on to oval-shaped pieces of card and join them at the base with a split-pin fastner to make the words 'sun' and 'sat'. Make one word fan for each pair of children. Write the letters 's', 'u', 'n', 's', 'a' and 't' on to individual sheets of A4 card. Write a large letter 's' and display it on the wall.

Theme links
Sound and rhythm
The alphabet
The weather

What to do
Ask the children to sit down on the floor facing you. Invite them to imagine that they are sitting on the beach on a lovely hot sunny day. Talk about the heat from the sun, and fan yourself with your hand to cool down. Explain that you want to make the word 'sun'. Show the children the large letter 's' on the wall. Say the 's' sound and ask what other sounds they can hear in the word 'sun'. Hand out the appropriate A4 letter cards, giving each card to a different child, and ask the children to stand in front of the group. Invite a volunteer to arrange the children, so that they are standing in the right order to make the word 'sun'.

Now hand the word fans to pairs of children and ask them to arrange the letters in the correct order to make the word 'sun', then hold them up. Repeat the activity with the word 'sat'.

Collect the fans back in, then hand them out randomly to the children. Ask those children holding the word 'sun' to stand up and shine down on those with the word 'sat'. The children sitting down can use their word fans to keep cool!

Support and extension
Younger children can concentrate on the 's' sound, matching it to the letter shape, writing the letter and thinking of words that start with that initial sound. Older children can copy the words on to paper and have a go at writing other words beginning with 's'.

Home partnership
Encourage parents and carers to help their children learn their letters by sharing alphabet books and puzzles with them at home.

Further ideas
♦ Make activity sheets with words and pictures of simple three-letter words, such as 'dog', 'cat', 'sun' and 'hat'. Leave the initial letter off the words for the children to write in.
♦ Make other word fans, perhaps with the children's names on.

Making waves

Stepping Stone
Use words and/or gestures, including body language such as eye contact and facial expression, to communicate.

Early Learning Goal
Interact with others, negotiating plans and activities and taking turns in conversation.

Group size
Up to four children.

What you need
Painting combs; water tray; small plastic boats; plastic drinking straws; tray of damp sand; paper; blue, white and green paint; photograph or illustration of a boat on a stormy sea.

Preparation
Prepare a painting table with plates of blue, white and green paint.

What to do

Begin by sharing the picture with the children. Ask them how they would feel if they were in that boat on the stormy sea. Would it be exciting or maybe a little bit frightening? Invite the children to demonstrate how they would feel by making an appropriate facial expression to indicate whether they would be happy and excited or a little bit scared. Explain that, when the wind blows on the sea it makes waves; the harder it blows the bigger the waves are.

Place a toy boat on the water tray and take turns to blow it across the water using the straw. Set up a race between two boats. Invite two children to each blow their boat across the water. Cheer them along and praise both children for their efforts. Ask them whether they enjoyed the race.

Now invite the children to work together to make wave patterns in the sand. How could they create the patterns? Perhaps they could use their fingers, or drag the combs through the sand. Encourage them to explain to you and to each other how they are making their patterns. When they have experimented freely making big and small waves, show them how to use the combs to make waves with paint on paper. Talk about the patterns. Are they trying to make little calm waves on the water, or big exciting ones? Use the opportunity to reinforce water safety and to remind children never to go near water without an adult.

Support and extension

Put some play people in the boats and ask younger children to tell you how they are feeling when the water is calm and then rough and stormy. Older children could draw pictures to show how the play people are feeling.

Home partnership

Encourage parents to watch or listen to weather forecasts at home with their children. Let the children talk about the forecasts back at your setting.

Further ideas

♦ Tell stories about adventures at the seaside or out at sea. Stop at relevant points and use facial expressions to demonstrate how the characters in the story are feeling.
♦ Develop the wave paintings into stormy day pictures. Encourage the children to talk about their pictures and tell stories about them.

Theme links
Ourselves
Patterns
Weather

Foundation Themes
The Seaside

Seaside music

Stepping Stone
Observe the effects of
activity on their bodies.

Early Learning Goal
Recognise the changes that
happen to their bodies when
they are active.

Group size
Up to eight
children.

What you need
Tape recorder or
CD player; tape
or CD of happy
lively music, such
as The Beach Boys
'Greatest Hits'
(Capitol); paper
plates; dried pasta;
stapler (adult use);
sticky tape; orange
and yellow paper;
scissors; glue;
pens.

Preparation
Cut out circles and
triangles from the
coloured paper to
make the suns and
sun rays. Make a
sun shaker. Stick
coloured triangles
around the edge
of one plate, and
a large circular
sun on the back
of the plate. Turn
the plate over and
put a small amount
of dried pasta
on it, then stick
another plate on
top, sandwiching
the edge of the
triangles and
pasta between the
two plates (see
illustration).

Theme links
Food
Ourselves
Sport

What to do

Talk about sunny days at the seaside.
Remind the children of fairground
rides and arcades that they might
see at the seaside and talk about the happy sounds and music that they might hear.
Now show them your sun shaker, and ask them to listen as you shake it. What can
they hear?

Tell the children that they are going to make their own sun shakers and enjoy
some seaside music. Give each child a paper plate and invite them to stick a sun
shape on it, then to draw on a smiling face. Show them how to stick triangles
around the edge. Now ask them to write their name on a second plate. Put a
handful of dried pasta into the centre of one paper plate, and staple the second
plate on top. Tape over the staples.

Sit in a circle with the sun shakers in front of you. Listen to the music you have
chosen, and invite the children to sing along with you. Encourage them to copy
you as you clap your hands or pat your knees to the rhythm of the music, then pick
up the instruments and play along together. Stand up and dance around the room,
shaking the sun shakers high in the air and low near the ground. Twist and turn and
dance until you are ready to stop.

After a few minutes, stop dancing. Stand still and listen to the sound of your
breath and feel the beat of your heart. Sit down and talk about the changes that
have taken place in your bodies as you danced around the room. Finish off by lying
quietly on the floor and feeling your breath and your heart slow down and your
body temperature cool.

Support and extension

Show younger children
where to put their hands to
feel their heart and lungs.
Show older children a
diagram of the body and
point out the heart and
lungs.

Home partnership

Talk about the different types
of exercise that the children
do at home. Encourage
parents to take their children
swimming.

Further ideas

♦ Hold races outside and
listen to your heart and
breath sounds.
♦ Find out about ways that
we can cool down when
we have been exercising.
Discuss the importance of
exercise and talk about the
children's favourite games
and sports.

Sounds of the sea

Group size
Up to eight children.

What you need
Small cardboard boxes; empty yoghurt pots; plastic bottles; egg-boxes; cylindrical containers; sandpaper; stones; dry sand; dried peas; lentils; rice; sticky tape; scissors; glue; CDs or tapes of sea and storm music, such as The Hebrides, 'Fingal's Cave' by Mendelssohn; CD player or tape recorder; flip chart; paper and pen; songs about the sea (see pages 86 to 88).

Preparation
Set out the containers and contents on a table.

What to do
Sit the children where they can listen comfortably to some sea and storm music. Explain that you would like them to think about the different sounds that they can hear. Listen to the music together, then ask the children about the sounds they heard. What did the sounds remind them of? What instruments might have been used to make the sounds? On the flip chart, make a list of sea sounds, such as the waves crashing, water trickling, sand crunching, pebbles rolling up and down the beach and the wind blowing.

Show the children the variety of containers and contents and explain that you would like some ideas and help to make instruments that you can use to re-create the sounds of the sea. Ask the children to examine the materials and have a go at making different sound effects.

Try filling containers with sand and pebbles to make the sound of waves crashing on the beach. Rice will make a gentler, softer sound when tipped up and down in a sealed container, while sheets of sandpaper rubbed together can be used for footsteps on the beach.

Ask the children to sit in a circle on the floor with their instrument in front of them. Explain the importance of keeping the instruments still when they are not being played. Ask one child at a time to play their instrument and the rest of the group to listen and suggest what seaside sound it reminds them of. Use the instruments to make seaside sounds as you sing a selection of songs about the sea.

Support and extension
Help younger children to make shakers by placing stones, sand, rice or lentils in a yoghurt pot and sealing the lid down. Each pot will make a different sound depending on the size and amount of contents. Ask older children to make an instrument to represent each of the sounds on your list.

Home partnership
Find out whether you have any musicians among your parents and carers. Ask them if they would come in and play for the children.

Further idea
♦ Use commercial percussion instruments and compare the sounds with the children's own creations.

Theme links
Materials
The senses

Chapter 2

On the beach

Enjoy finding out about things that people do on the beach with the activities in this chapter. There are ideas for making your own sand sculptures, creating some textured sandpaper letters and exploring the properties of sand, plus imaginative ways to use your beachcombing treasures.

Group size
Whole group.

What you need
A picture of a donkey; coconut shells or a wood-block; the poem 'Donkey rides' on the photocopiable sheet on page 83.

Riding on a donkey

What to do
Show the children the picture of the donkey. Does anyone know where donkeys usually live? Why do we sometimes see them at the seaside? Explain that some seaside resorts have donkey rides on the beach. Children can buy a ticket and ride up and down the sand on a donkey. These donkeys usually live near the beach in summer.

Ask the children to suggest what might happen to the donkeys when the summer is over. Where do they go? Who looks after them? Do they think the donkeys enjoy taking children for rides along the beach? Ask if any of the children have ever ridden on a donkey or a horse. Where else have the children seen donkeys, apart from the beach? Talk about the things that a donkey would need to help him stay happy and healthy, such as a warm place to sleep, enough food and plenty of space to run around.

Read the donkey rhyme through twice and encourage the children to join in. Use coconut shells or a woodblock to make the sound of the donkey's feet and play along to the rhyme. Encourage the children to join in by patting their knees or clapping in time to the rhythm.

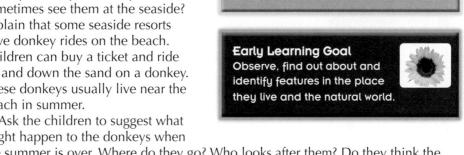

Stepping Stone
Show an interest in the world in which they live.

Early Learning Goal
Observe, find out about and identify features in the place they live and the natural world.

Support and extension
Ask adult helpers to sit with younger children and help them to clap and pat in time to the rhythm. Let older children use woodblocks once they have mastered the rhythm.

Home partnership
Invite parents and carers to come and listen to the children recite the donkey poem. Add a few seaside songs and hold a short performance.

Further ideas
♦ Share books and the children's own experiences about seaside activities and games.
♦ Ask the children about other activities that they might do on or around the beach, such as play with a ball or visit an aquarium.

Theme links
Animals
Nursery rhymes
Places around us

She sells sea shells

Stepping Stone
Further explore an experience using a range of senses.

Early Learning Goal
Respond in a variety of ways to what they see, hear, smell, touch and feel.

Group size
Up to ten children.

What you need
A basket of shells (from existing collections); wax crayons; pastels; chalks; thin white paper; a transparent container; water.

Preparation
Fill a transparent container half-full of water (or enough to cover the shells).

What to do

Sit the children together in a circle and show them the basket of shells. Explain that shells were once the homes of animals and we can often find them washed up on the beach. Ask the children if they have ever walked along the beach looking for shells.

Choose and describe one of the shells and pass it around the group. Invite the children to look at both sides of the shell, feel each surface and describe the textures, shapes and colours. Look for shells that are unusual shapes, such as fans or spirals. Encourage the children to describe the shapes and compare them to objects that they are familiar with.

When you have passed a variety of shells around the group, gather them back and place them carefully into a bowl of water. Ask the children to watch what happens. Do they float or sink? What happens to the colours of the shells? Remove the shells from the water and ask the children to point out and describe their favourites. Talk about the creatures that lived in the shells, and discuss how the shells might have ended up on the beach.

Finish the session by making drawings and paintings of the shells. Take wax rubbings of the flatter shells, painting a thin colour wash over the top. Use the pastels and chalks to draw the other shells, mixing colours to make them as lifelike as possible. Display your pictures on the wall for everyone to enjoy.

Support and extension

Help the younger children to think of simple words to describe and compare the shells. Ask older children to think of more complex words to describe the shapes, textures and patterns on the shells.

Home partnership

Ask the children to bring in contributions from home for a collection of sea shells, rocks and corals.

Further ideas

♦ Place some items with contrasting textures in a cloth bag. Pass the bag around and ask the children to feel for rough and smooth objects. Sort other items into sets of shiny and dull or hard and soft.
♦ Make a viewer from a clear plastic bottle with the bottom cut off. Stretch cling film across the bottom and tape it in place. Push the viewer through the surface of the water and describe the shells that you can see.

Theme links
Colours
Materials
Senses
Shapes

Foundation Themes
The Seaside

Footprints in the sand

Stepping Stone
Notice and comment on patterns.

Early Learning Goal
Look closely at similarities, differences, patterns and change.

Group size
Up to eight children.

What you need
The 'Whose footprint?' photocopiable sheet on page 92; red or blue paint; shallow tray; paintbrush; large sheets of paper; bowl of soapy water; paper towels.

Preparation
Mix up some thick blue or red paint and pour it into a shallow tray. Place the paper next to the paint tray. Place the bowl of soapy water on the floor with the paper towels nearby.

What to do

Ask the children to imagine that they are walking along a sandy beach. What would they leave behind as they walked? Explain that when we walk on the sand, we leave a trail of footprints that show exactly where we have stepped. Show the children the pictures of the different footprints in the sand from the photocopiable sheet. Can anyone suggest what type of creature made each of the different footprints?

Once you have sorted out and identified each print, encourage the children to take off their shoes and socks and look at their own feet. What sort of footprint would they leave if they walked on the sand? Try to find the correct print from the selection that you have just been looking at. Discuss the different parts of the children's feet and count how many toes they have.

One at a time, invite each child to tread in a tray of paint and then carefully step on to the paper to make footprints. Talk about the activity as you do it; what does the paint feel like between the children's toes? Does sand feel the same when we walk on it?

As you carefully wash and dry each child's feet, ask them what the water and paper towel feel like against their feet. When the footprints are dry, cut them out and display on the wall in pairs.

Support and extension

Let younger children match their prints to their foot to see if they are the same size and shape. Older children can sort the footprints in order of length, then see if the longer feet belong to the taller children.

Home partnership

Encourage parents and carers to try using finger-paints at home with their children. Suggest that they do the activity outside and enjoy making pictures using their fingers, hands and feet!

Further ideas

♦ Make wet footprints outside on the concrete on a hot sunny day. Watch the water evaporate and the footprints disappear.
♦ Discuss what happens when the waves come up the beach and wash over the sand.
♦ Give each child a copy of the 'Whose footprint?' photocopiable sheet. Invite them to press different items into a tray of wet sand to try to make the different footprint shapes.

Theme links
Opposites
Patterns
Shapes and sizes

Ten plastic buckets

Group size
Up to ten children.

What you need
A pen; ten plastic buckets of different colours, shapes and sizes; ten sticky labels, numbered 1 to 10.

Preparation
Line up the buckets on a table or shelf.

What to do
Talk to the children about the games and activities that they like to play at the seaside. Does anyone like to build sand-castles or dig trenches? What would they need to take with them to have fun digging in the sand? Show the children your line of buckets, and explain that you are going to sing a song about them. Sit the children on the floor in front of the buckets and count them together. Sing a version of the song 'Ten Green Bottles' (Traditional) together, encouraging the children to join in as you sing 'Ten Plastic Buckets Sitting on the Beach'. As you sing, ask a different child each time to remove the last bucket from the end of the row.

Place the buckets back in a line. Encourage the children to point out individual buckets by asking them questions about the colour and position of different buckets. For example, can they point out the red bucket? What is the colour of the second bucket? Give each child a numbered sticker and ask them to help you label the buckets, then line them up in the correct numerical order.

Muddle up some of the buckets and see if the children can spot and correct the mistakes that you have made. Sing the song through once more together. Each time a child removes the last bucket from the end of the row, pause in your singing to count how many buckets are left. Finish by looking at your collection of buckets. Ask the children some questions to reinforce the learning. For example, if you removed one of the blue buckets, how many would you have left? How many more red buckets would you need to make a total of five?

Support and extension
Help the younger children by numbering the buckets first and simplifying the questions. For older children turn the buckets around so that the stickers are hidden and ask them to identify, for example, bucket number 2 or number 8.

Home partnership
Ask parents and carers to sing number rhymes or play counting games at home with their children.

Further ideas
♦ Give each child a numbered bucket and encourage them to count the correct number of shells into it.
♦ Sing the song 'My bucket is full of things I found' on the photocopiable sheet on page 86.
♦ Encourage older children to estimate the total number of shells in two buckets. Tip them out and count them back into the buckets to check.

Theme links
Number rhymes
Toys

What's inside?

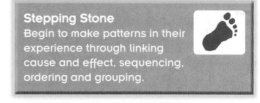

Stepping Stone
Begin to make patterns in their experience through linking cause and effect, sequencing, ordering and grouping.

Early Learning Goal
Use talk to organise, sequence and clarify thinking, ideas, feelings and events.

Group size
Whole group.

What you need
A child's plastic bucket; small seaside objects, such as a shell, a pebble and a toy fish.

Preparation
Hide one of the small items in the bucket.

What to do
Sit the children on the floor next to you and show them your bucket. Pretend that you have been down to the beach and have hidden a seaside treasure in your bucket. Ask for a volunteer to come up and help you. Allow your helper to hold the bucket and look inside, but not to tell the other children what it is. Explain to the rest of the group that you would like them to try to guess what is in the bucket by asking your helper questions. Begin by asking the first question yourself. Ask about the colour of the object, its shape, its size, its function and the letter sound that it begins with. As the game goes on, the children will start to ask more relevant questions and build up their questioning skills.

Replace the objects once the children have guessed what they are, and make sure that all of the children have an opportunity to ask and answer questions.

Keep the session short, but repeat it on a regular basis. See how many questions the children need to ask each time before they can guess the hidden treasure! Help them to think logically and ask sensible questions.

Support and extension
For younger children, ask another adult to join in and ask the questions, but let the children do the guessing. Let older children take turns at hiding their own choice of treasure and being the question master.

Home partnership
Ask parents and carers to play guessing games, such as 'I spy', with their children at home and on journeys.

Further idea
♦ Line up several buckets and place a different seaside object in each one. Make sure you name the objects and show them to the children before you put them into the buckets, then see how many of the objects they can remember.

Theme links
Puzzles
Shapes

Foundation
Themes
The Seaside

Sandpaper letters

Early Learning Goal
Use a pencil and hold it effectively to form recognisable letters, most of which are correctly formed.

Group size
Up to four children.

What you need
Sheets of fairly coarse sandpaper; lower-case letter templates; card; scissors; PVA glue; tray of damp sand; a cup of dry sand; alphabet book or frieze; sugar paper; brushes; pencils; paper.

Preparation
Choosing letters that are relevant to the seaside work that you are doing with your group, cut out one or more letter shapes from the sandpaper (A4 size or smaller) and mount on a piece of card.

What to do
Show the children a sheet of sandpaper. Can anyone tell you what it is? What is it made from? What do they think it might be used for? Explain that the paper has lots of tiny grains of sand on it, just like the sand that we find on the beach! Let the children touch the sandpaper. Does it feel like the sand that we sit on at the beach?

Sing an alphabet song together or share an alphabet book or frieze with the children, familiarising them with the letter names. Choose a letter and ask the children if they recognise it. Show the children your pre-cut sandpaper letters, and name each one together. One at a time, show the children how to form the letter by placing their index finger in the correct starting place on the sandpaper and then tracing the shape. Do this a couple of times and then invite the children to try it on their own.

Move over to the sand tray and encourage the children to write the letter in the sand using their index finger. See if they can tell you what sound the letter makes and then name something that has that initial sound.

Let the children have a go at making their own sandpaper letters. Encourage them to dip a brush into watered-down PVA glue and paint their choice of letter on to sugar paper. Let them sprinkle dry sand over their letter, then shake off the excess. How do their letters compare with your sandpaper letters? Finally ask the children to have a go at writing the letter with pencil and paper.

Support and extension
Encourage younger children to close their eyes while you draw the letter on to their hand with your finger. With older children, draw the same letter on to their backs, and see if they can recognise the shape of the letter. They can try this on each other once they feel confident.

Home partnership
Ask parents and carers to help their children to cut out the letters of their names from sandpaper to use as nameplates on their bedroom doors.

Further ideas
♦ Compare the textures of sandpaper, wet sand and dry sand.
♦ Make seaside collage pictures, using pieces of sandpaper to represent the beach and sandcastles.

Theme links
Materials
Senses

Sandy souvenirs

Early Learning Goal
Explore colour, texture, shape, form and space in two or three dimensions.

What to do

Talk with the children about the different types of shops that you might find at the beach. Ask whether anyone has ever bought any souvenirs of their holiday from a shop at the seaside. What did they buy? Explain that in seaside souvenir shops, people often buy pictures made from sand or little bottles filled with coloured sand, to remind them of their seaside holiday.

Invite the children to make their own seaside souvenir pictures. Show them the glitter, and point out that it is made up of tiny pieces, just like sand. Pass around the pot of sand and dry powder paint and ask the children if they can guess what it is. Explain that only very dry sand and powder paint can be used to sprinkle. What would happen if you added water to the sand and powder paint? Could you still sprinkle it then?

Draw a wavy line on to a piece of sugar paper and invite the children to watch while you spread glue over the line with a paintbrush, working from left to right across the page. Sprinkle the coloured sand over the glue using a spoon. Shake off the excess on to the newspaper and look at the patterns that you have made.

One at a time, help the children to make their own wave patterns, remembering to work from left to right and from top to bottom to cover the page. Leave the pictures to dry, then let the children feel the wave patterns they have made by gently running their fingers over the surface. Ask them what their waves feel like and encourage them to explain how they made them.

Support and extension

For younger children, put the sand and paint in a small container with a lid. Perforate the lid with holes and use as a shaker. Let older children try using the technique to write their own names.

Home partnership

Suggest that parents and carers work with their children to make simple collages from various seaside souvenirs including sand, shells and small pebbles.

Further idea

♦ Mix individual bowls of sand with different-coloured powder paint and glitter to make lots of different shades. Pour layers of coloured and glittery sand into small glass bottles or jars to make seaside souvenirs. Ask the children what would happen if you shook the jar.

Sand sculptures

Group size
Two children.

What you need
One tray of wet sand and one of dry sand; collection of sieves, spoons, funnels and moulds; bucket; sand wheels and scoops; a copy of the 'Wet or dry?' photocopiable sheet on page 93; clipboard; pencil.

Preparation
Give the children plenty of opportunity to play freely with the sand and sand toys for several sessions before you plan this activity. Attach the photocopiable sheet to the clipboard.

What to do
Talk with the children about times when they have played on the sand at the beach. What did they build with the sand? Did they use wet or dry sand to build sand-castles? Why? Tell the children that you are going to find out about the different things that you can do with sand when it is dry and when it is wet.

Invite the children over to the sand trays. Ask the children whether they think each tray contains wet or dry sand. Invite them to put their hands into the sand in each tray to make sure. Discuss the dangers of throwing sand and rubbing sand into your eyes. Remind the children that it is important to play considerately and to keep the sand in the sand tray, away from their own and their partner's face.

Give one child the clipboard and the other the pencil. Look at the pictures and the boxes that say 'wet' and 'dry'. Now look at the first picture on the sheet: a funnel with sand running through it. Try pouring wet sand through the funnel. Does it work? Draw a sad face in the 'wet' box to show that it does not work. Next try the dry sand. Can they pour this through the funnel? Draw a smiley face in the 'dry' box to show that you can pour dry sand through the funnel. Work through all the pictures, testing first with wet sand and then with dry sand, and filling in the 'wet' and 'dry' boxes accordingly.

Talk about the results on the sheet. See if the children can remember what could be done with the wet and dry sand, and encourage them to discuss the different properties. Finish the activity by letting the children play freely together in the wet and dry sand.

Support and extension
Help younger children to look at and feel the differences between the wet and dry sand. Encourage them to use words like 'sticky' and 'rough' to describe the sand. Older children can put ticks and crosses in the boxes, instead of faces. Encourage them to discuss what happens to the dry sand when water is added to it.

Home partnership
Ask the children if they have a sand-pit at home, or have been to a beach. Encourage individuals to bring in photographs if possible, and share their experiences with the rest of the group.

Further ideas
♦ Make a large sand sculpture in your outdoor sand-pit. Invite the children to choose a shape to make, such as a big fish or a mermaid, and to add their own smaller sculptures around the main sculpture.
♦ Make sand towers using very wet sand. Use a cupped hand to dribble it from a height, and see who can make the highest tower!

Theme links
Buildings and structures
How things work
Senses
Textures

Digging for treasure

Early Learning Goal
Use language such as 'greater', 'smaller', 'heavier' or 'lighter' to compare quantities.

Group size
Two children.

What you need
A bucket balance; sand tray; small plastic seaside toys; coloured stickers.

Preparation
Set up the bucket balance on a table next to the sand tray. Put a different coloured sticker or smiley face on each bucket. Bury some sorting toys in the sand.

What to do
Ask the children if they have ever dug for treasure on the beach. Tell them that there is some treasure buried in the sand tray and encourage them to come and dig in the sand to see what they can find. Show them the bucket balance next to the sand tray and position it so that each child is standing next to one of the buckets. Point out the coloured stickers and remind them which bucket they are to use. Stress the importance of working together, sharing the balance and taking turns.

Invite the first child to dig for an item of treasure and place it in the bucket on their side of the balance. What happens to the bucket balance? Can they tell you why the buckets are no longer level? Now let the second child dig for a piece of treasure and place it in their side of the balance. What happens to the balance this time? As each child finds another piece of treasure, talk about the movement of the balance and the number of treasure items being put in. Ask the children if they can think of a way to make the buckets move up and down.

Let the children play freely with the balance, noting their understanding of the concept of balance as well as their ability to share and take turns.

Support and extension
For younger children keep the activity short and concentrate on the words 'up' and 'down', 'heavy' and 'light'. Older children can think about how many pieces of treasure they will need to put in each side to make the buckets balance, and what will happen if they add or remove one piece.

Home partnership
Suggest that parents and carers provide balances and containers so that their children can compare quantities in their own sand-pits at home.

Further ideas
♦ Place a number flag in the sand tray. Invite two children to dig for that amount of treasure. Encourage them to count the number of treasures they have as they find each piece. Is it the same as the number on the flag or do they need more?
♦ Encourage the children to bury different pieces of treasure for a friend to find, giving clues to the location in the sand tray.

Theme links
Counting rhymes
Places around us

Beach collages

Group size
Two or three children.

What you need
An area of flat, damp sand (this could be in your sand-pit, or, if possible, on a beach); tray or table; natural objects such as shells, pebbles, driftwood and seaweed.

Preparation
Prepare the sand by flattening and smoothing the surface. Place the natural objects on a table or tray close by.

What to do
Ask the children if they have ever made pictures in the sand. What did they use to make the pictures? Did they draw in the sand with their fingers, or did they drag a stick or spade across it? Perhaps they added details and features to their pictures using shells or flags? Invite the children to have a go at making patterns in the sand using their fingers. Now show the children the natural objects, and suggest that you work together to make a picture using these.

Start by drawing the outline of a face. Encourage the children to choose suitable natural objects to add features, such as eyes, nose, mouth, eyebrows, hair and so on, to make a smiley face. Demonstrate how the picture can be altered by moving the objects around. Move a few objects to make your sand person sad. Ask the children why the sand person might be sad. Perhaps he is lonely or has sand in his eyes? Ask them to think of a way to cheer him up, then invite them to change the face and make it happy again. Try making other expressions, then remove all the items, smooth the sand over and let the children make pictures of their own.

Encourage them to talk about the pictures they are making and the items that they are using. Explain that on the beach, the tide comes in and washes the sand clear so that every day there is a fresh surface to create a picture on. Smooth over the surface of the pictures and start again!

Support and extension
Invite younger children to find their own natural items to make features on the face outline. Older children could find extra items to add to their picture, and frame their pictures with a repeating pattern of shells and stones.

Home partnership
Take some photographs of your sand collages before they are smoothed over and put them on display for parents and carers to see.

Further ideas
◆ Use stiff paper and strong glue to make a permanent collage using a selection of the natural items.
◆ Cut pictures of facial features from magazines. Move them around on a piece of paper to make changing expressions before sticking them down.
◆ Provide safety mirrors and let the children practise changing their own facial expressions.

Theme links
Changes
Ourselves
Senses

Sand patterns

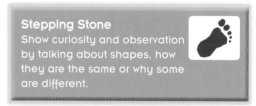
Early Learning Goal
Use language such as 'circle' or 'bigger' to describe the shape and size of solids and flat shapes.

Group size
Up to six children.

What you need
An empty, dry washing-up liquid bottle; dry sand; dry powder paint; bradawl or scissors (adult use); string; large sheets of paper; pictures of patterns left in the sand by the sea; sticky tape.

Preparation
Cut the bottom off and remove the stopper from the washing-up liquid bottle. Use the bradawl or scissors to make a hole in either side of the bottle at the base, then thread a long piece of string through so that it can be suspended upside-down. Replace the stopper, then half-fill the bottle with a mixture of dry sand and powder paint. Suspend the bottle from the ceiling, within the children's reach. Spread the paper on the floor and tape them together.

Theme links
Colours
Movement
Shapes

What to do
Talk about the sea with the children. Has anyone ever noticed what happens to the sand when the tide goes out? If possible, show the children pictures of the wavy line patterns that are left in the sand when the tide goes out. Explain that the movement of the water pushes the sand into little peaks, which make wavy patterns. Invite the children to create their own patterns with sand.

Ask the children to come and look at the sand-filled bottle. What do they think will happen if you give the bottle a push? Invite one child to demonstrate. Now point out the coloured sand in the bottle. What would happen if you took the lid off the bottle? Remove the lid and again invite a child to swing the bottle. Enjoy watching the sand create pretty patterns on the floor.

Try making different patterns by swinging the bottle backwards and forwards, or round and round. Encourage the children to describe the different patterns that they are making. Can they make a wavy pattern, just like the ripples that the sea leaves in the sand at the seaside? Show the children how to scoop the sand up and pour it back into the bottle, then have fun making more patterns on the paper.

Support and extension
Help younger children to see how they can push the bottle harder to make longer shapes. Challenge older children to link the patterns that they make to the movement of the bottle. What happens when the bottle slows down?

Home partnership
Encourage parents and carers to try using straws and runny poster paint with their children to blow water patterns across paper.

Further ideas
♦ Put paint into the bottle instead of sand, and make permanent patterns.
♦ Suspend several bottles from the ceiling, each full of different-coloured sand or paint. Enjoy making a large-scale group pattern picture.

Beachcombers

Group size
Up to ten children.

What you need
Seaside items from existing collections, such as shells, pebbles, dried seaweed and driftwood; small box; books or posters about sea life, such as Life in...A Rockpool on the Seashore by Sally Morgan (Belitha Press); clipboards; paper; pencils.

Preparation
Place the seaside items in the box. Prepare a nature walk sheet relevant to your own local area, with drawings of items that the children are likely to see, such as a tree, flower, bird, leaf, pebble, bark, twig and snail. Photocopy one sheet per group.

Theme links
Animals
Our world
Places around us
Plants

What to do

Sit the children in a circle and tip out the box of seaside items on to the floor. Ask the children where they think you might have found these items. See how many they can name.

Explain that none of the items in your collection are alive. Now ask the children to see how many creatures they can think of that live in the sea. Look at posters and picture books, and see how many more you can name. Emphasise the importance of leaving living things where they belong. Tell the children that, although it is nice to look at crabs, starfish and other creatures on the beach, we must always put them back where we found them.

Ask the children if they would like to join you on a nature walk. Tell them that you have some pictures of items they might see on their walk. Explain that if they see any of the items on the sheet they can circle them with a pencil. Show them the pictures and ask them to help you identify them before you set off.

Divide the children into small groups with one clipboard and picture sheet per group. During the walk remind the children not to pick flowers or collect items. Instead they should just point them out and mark them off on their sheet.

Back at your setting, look at the sheets and discuss what you saw and where you saw it. Ask the children if they enjoyed the walk. Can they think of any other things that they saw that were not on the sheet?

Support and extension

With younger children, ask an adult to hold the clipboard and circle the objects when the children point them out. Older children can work in pairs with a clipboard between them.

Home partnership

Let the children take their nature walk sheets home. Encourage parents and carers to ask their children about the things that they saw on their walk.

Further ideas

♦ Discuss the dangers of leaving litter on the beach, explaining that it can be harmful to people and animals. Remind the children that they should always put their litter in the bin or take it home with them.
♦ During circle time, imagine that you are taking a walk along a beach. Make a list of all the creatures and plants that you might see.

Chapter 3

Seaside games

In this chapter, children will enjoy making and playing all sorts of exciting seaside games. Develop positional language by following a trail of footprints in the sand, try your hand at magnetic fishing and pretend to manoeuvre your way around a perilous cliff-top trail!

Catch of the day

Group size
Two children at a time.

What you need
Coloured card; two horseshoe magnets; string; sticky tape; two rods made from dowel or garden cane; two buckets; a large plastic hoop; giant metal paper clips; sticky labels.

Preparation
Draw and cut out ten card fish, 10cm long, from coloured card. Write a number from 1 to 10 on the back. Check that rods are splinter free and smooth-ended. Tie each horseshoe magnet to a length of string and attach to each rod with sticky tape. Attach a paper clip to each fish.

Theme links
Food
How things work
Materials

What to do
Ask the children if they have ever been fishing. Talk about the different ways that you can catch fish, for example, using a fishing rod or a net. Show them the rods that you have made. Explain that magnets will pick up metal objects, and demonstrate by 'catching' a fish with a paper clip attached to it.

Place all the fish inside a plastic hoop on the floor, explaining that the hoop is the 'sea'. Invite one of the children to try to catch a fish with the magnetic rod. Now ask them to remove the paper clips and say what they think will happen when they try to catch the fish this time.

Give each child a magnetic rod and a bucket, then let the children take turns to catch the fish. Each time they catch one, ask them to say the number on the fish, then place it in their bucket. When all the fish have been caught ask the children to count them and see whether they both have the same amount. See if they can tell you how they caught the fish. Let the children tip their fish back into the 'sea'. Now label each child's bucket with a number. Challenge each child to say the number on their bucket, and to catch the same number of fish from the 'sea'. Each time they catch a fish, ask the children to say how many they have caught and how many more they will need to make the number on their bucket. Play several times, varying the numbers on the buckets each time.

Stepping Stone
Talk about what is seen and what is happening.

Early Learning Goal
Ask questions about why things happen and how things work.

Support and extension
For younger children, work with numbers to five. Let older children make other sea creatures to catch with their magnetic rods. Include starfish, octopuses, seahorses and maybe some sharks!

Home partnership
Encourage parents and carers to explain to their children how the fish that they see in the supermarkets is caught.

Further idea
♦ Blu-Tack your numbered fish in order on the wall to make a fish number line.

Swim, little fishy

Stepping Stone
Value and contribute to own well-being and self-control.

Early Learning Goal
Work as part of a group or class, taking turns and sharing fairly, understanding that there needs to be agreed values and codes of behaviour for groups of people, including adults and children, to work together harmoniously.

Group size
Up to four children.

What you need
Large plastic hoop; set of laminated fish cards numbered 1 to 10; set of number cards from 1 to 10.

Preparation
Place the hoop on the floor to make a 'rock pool' and put some of the fish carefully inside it so that they do not touch each other. Place the number cards on the floor outside the hoop.

What to do

Ask the children to stand in an open space. Encourage them to spread their arms out to make sure that they are not touching the person next to them. Pretend that you are all little fish, swimming around in a rock pool. As you flit around, try hard to avoid bumping into the 'fish' next to you! Enjoy swimming in and around each other, and greeting each other as you pass.

Now invite the children to come and sit by the 'rock pool'. Explain that the fish in the rock pool are enjoying swimming around with their friends, just as you have all been doing. Ask the children to guess how many fish are in the rock pool. Count the fish by touching each one and moving them to one side of the pool. Repeat the final number and ask one of the children to find the number card to match from the selection next to the rock pool.

Take out or add a few fish and then ask a child to count the fish and find the correct number card. Repeat the activity, giving each child a chance to count the fish and find the card. When everyone has had a turn, change the activity by putting a number card in the rock pool and asking the children to count the correct number of fish into the pool.

Support and extension

For younger children, work with numbers up to 5. Ask older children addition and subtraction questions. For example: 'If one fish swam away, how many would be left?'; 'If one more fish came along to join his friends, how many would there be?'.

Home partnership

Provide a zip wallet with a set of laminated fish and a set of number cards for a child to borrow. Include a sheet of game suggestions for counting, addition and subtraction.

Further ideas

♦ Say together the counting rhyme 'How many fishes?' on the photocopiable sheet on page 84.
♦ Sing 'One, Two, Three, Four, Five, Once I Caught a Fish Alive'.

Theme links
Movement
Number rhymes
Our friends

Foundation
Themes
The Seaside

Sharks!

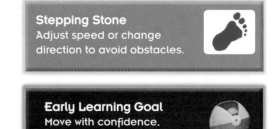

Stepping Stone
Adjust speed or change direction to avoid obstacles.

Early Learning Goal
Move with confidence, imagination and in safety.

Group size
Whole group.

What you need
Plastic hoops (one less than the number of children in your group); a tambourine; large indoor or outdoor area; information books with pictures of fish and sharks, such as Shark by Miranda MacQuitty and John Woodcock (Dorling Kindersley).

Preparation
Place the hoops on the floor or grass.

What to do

Talk about the fish that live in the sea. Explain that some fish are tiny, while others are much bigger and more powerful. Share the books with the children, and talk about the difference in size between the fish and the sharks. Explain that the sharks eat the smaller fish, who have to try to swim away very fast to avoid being eaten!

Show the children the hoops on the ground. Tell them that you would like them to imagine that the ground is the sea and the hoops are islands. Invite the children to pretend to be fish swimming in and out of the islands as you play the tambourine.

Once they have warmed up explain that you are a shark and you are going to try to catch them for your tea! When you shake the tambourine they must swim in and out of the hoop islands, and when you bang it they have to swim to an island where they will be safe from the shark. There is one problem though – only one fish is allowed on each island. Start shaking the tambourine and join the fish in the 'sea' as you swim around together. When you bang the tambourine, pretend to catch the fish that did not make it to an island. This lucky fish gets to be a shark with you next time, as you shake the tambourine.

Support and extension

With younger children, put out one hoop per child and let them enjoy swimming between the islands without getting caught. With older children, have just half the number of hoops for the number of children in your group. Explain that two fish can hide on each island.

Home partnership

Explain the game to parents and carers and suggest that they play it at home with their children on a smaller scale.

Further ideas

♦ Let the children take turns to be the shark, fishing for its tea.
♦ Give each child a coloured sash, and challenge them to swim to the hoop that matches their coloured sash when you bang the tambourine.

Theme links
Journeys
Movement
Shape and space

Foundation Themes
The Seaside

Catch the fish

Stepping Stone
Manage body to create intended movements.

Early Learning Goal
Move with control and co-ordination.

Group size
Whole group.

What you need
Ribbon, scarves or sashes to tie around the children's waists (ensure that you have enough for half of the children in your group); information books containing pictures of seals, such as Wild Britain: Animals–Seal by Louise and Richard Spilsbury (Heinemann Library).

What to do

Begin by sharing the information books with the children. Talk about the graceful way that the seals dive beneath the waves and swim through the sea. Can anyone suggest what sort of food the seals eat? If necessary, explain that they catch fish in the sea.

Tell the children that you are going to play a game of fish and seals; some of them are going to be fish, and some are going to be seals, looking for some food to eat. Divide the children into two groups. Help each of the children in one group to tie a sash around their waists. Stress that they must only tie the sashes loosely around their waists and nowhere else. Tell this group that they are going to be the fish. Ask the rest of the children, the seals, to sit down. Invite the fish to swim in and around them, then swap over and let the seals swim around the fish. Encourage each group to move appropriately; the fish might dart around or swim together in shoals, while the seals could glide gracefully as if they are diving beneath the waves and swimming underwater. Ask everyone to sit down again and to listen carefully while you explain how to play 'Catch the fish'.

When you say, 'Swim', all the fish should swim away while the seals swim after them, trying to catch them. If they catch a fish they should hold hands with them and stand still. Keep the game short and stop after a few minutes by shouting, 'Freeze'. Ask the children to help you to count how many fish have not been caught and are still swimming in the sea. Suggest that the children swap over so that the fish have a turn at being seals.

At the end of the game ask all the children to sit down and relax. Ask them what it felt like being a fish trying to escape from a hungry seal. Did they prefer to be a fish or a seal?

Support and extension

Provide adult helpers to support younger children on both teams. For older children, keep the game going longer and see if the seals can catch all the fish.

Home partnership

Ask parents for spare scarves and sashes that can be used for games, dance and role-play. Invite them to join in with the 'Catch the fish' game.

Further ideas

♦ Make the game more exciting by playing some lively music as the seals try to catch the fish.
♦ Watch videos of seals swimming in the sea and try to copy their graceful movements.

Theme links
Animals
Movement
Our world

Follow the footprints

Stepping Stone
Show confidence in linking up with others for support and guidance.

Early learning Goal
Maintain attention, concentrate, and sit quietly when appropriate.

Group size
Up to four children.

What you need
A4 paper; pencil; laminating materials; scissors; a box of 'treasure' (chocolate coins, home-made bangles or cards with 'well done' written on them); blue and yellow fabric.

Preparation
Draw around your bare foot, then cut out ten or more paper footprints. Laminate them so that they can be used again. Set out a trail of laminated footprints in a safe area of your setting leading to some 'treasure'. Use chairs, tables and other furniture that the child can safely climb over, under and around. Place the yellow fabric on the floor, and use it to cover some of the furniture to represent a sandy beach and dunes. Lay the blue fabric on the floor to represent the sea.

What to do

Begin by telling the children a simple story about a pirate searching for buried treasure. Explain that the pirate followed a trail of footprints in the sand, which led him to the exact spot where the treasure was buried. When he dug deep down into the sand, he found a treasure chest full of chocolate coins!

Talk about times when the children have walked on the beach. Encourage them to share their experiences of leaving footprints in the wet sand. Now explain that, somewhere in your room, there is a hidden treasure chest. To find it, the children will have to follow a trail of footprints, just like the pirate did. Encourage the children to listen and watch very carefully as you follow the footprints first, making your way slowly along the trail and using positional language as you describe each step. For example: 'I'm following the footsteps *around* the edge of the water, *inside* a cave, *over* a soft, sandy dune, *behind* a palm tree...'

At the end of the trail pick up the treasure and return to the beginning to show the children your bounty. Ask each child in turn to hide the treasure and set out the footsteps, so that they lead to the treasure, passing in and out of the beach scene in a winding route. They can then invite another child to follow the trail and try to find the treasure, while the rest of the group remains seated and helps you to describe the trail that the child is taking.

Support and extension

Walk along the trail with younger children, holding their hand and emphasising the positional language. Give older children a map with directional clues on to help them find the treasure.

Home partnership

Let the children take their treasure home and explain to their parents how they found it. Encourage parents and carers to set up similar trails for their children.

Further ideas

♦ Sing the song 'Your footprints' on the photocopiable sheet on page 87.
♦ Write a number on each of the laminated footprints and encourage children to arrange them in numerical order.
♦ Make treasure maps showing the location of treasure buried in the sand tray.

Theme links
Journeys
Opposites
Places around us

Castle challenge

Stepping Stone
Sustain interest for a length of time on a pre-decided construction or arrangement.

Early Learning Goal
Use developing mathematical ideas and methods to solve practical problems.

Group size
Four or five children.

What you need
A one-minute sand-timer; thin coloured card; glue; A4 white card; scissors; bowls.

Preparation
Draw and cut out the outline of a flat-topped sand-castle from yellow card. Cut out individual yellow turrets that will fit on top of the sand-castle. Cut a sun from orange card, a flag from blue card and a shell from red card. Prepare one picture to show where each of the pieces goes (see illustration). Stick the pieces down on the card. Make sure you have enough pieces for each child to make a complete picture. Put the pieces in individual bowls.

What to do
Show the children the sand-timer and ask them if they know what it is. Tip it up and watch together as the sand run through. Tell them that the sand-timer contains thousands of tiny grains of sand, just like the sand that the children play with on the beach. Notice the little space that the sand pours through. Explain that it takes exactly one minute for the sand to run through from one end to the other. Ask the children to keep their eyes shut while you tip the sand-timer up again and to put their hands up when they think the sand has run through and one minute is up.

Now tell the children that you are going to play a game using the sand-timer. Show them your finished picture, and explain that they are going to make similar pictures, but they only have one minute in which to do them! Show the children the individual bowls of pieces, and demonstrate how they can be put together on a sheet of card to make a complete picture.

Turn the timer over and say, 'Go'. The children should start by finding the outline of the castle from the pieces in the bowls, then add the turrets, the flag and finally the sun and the shell. When the timer has run out, say, 'Stop', and see who has completed most of their picture.

Turn the timer over and play again, challenging the children to complete their picture before the minute is up. Finally, let the children stick their pieces down to make a permanent picture. Name them and display them on the wall.

Support and extension
Give younger children the pieces that they will need for their picture before you turn the timer over, so they do not have to find them in the bowls. Older children could take turns turning over the timer and saying, 'Go' and, 'Stop'.

Home partnership
Ask parents to play timed activities at home with their children. Provide ideas for games and, if necessary, let children borrow the sand-timer.

Further ideas
♦ Use the timer for other activities, such as making a real sand-castle in the sand tray, or finding buried plastic sea creatures.
♦ Number the pieces of the sand-castle and encourage the children to complete their pictures by placing the correct pieces in numerical sequence.

Theme links
Buildings
Changes
Games

Guess the shape

What to do

Ask the children if they like playing in the sand, both on the beach and in sand-pits. Talk about digging in the sand and building sand-castles and ask them if they have ever buried their legs in the sand at the beach or in a sand-pit. Explain that you have buried some sea animals in the sand tray. Invite them to have a look. Can they see anything peeping out of the sand? Encourage them to guess which animals are hidden, without touching them. Can they explain their answers? For example, perhaps they can see part of a star shape, so they think it is a starfish that is buried in the sand. Let one child pull an animal out of the sand and see if anyone has guessed correctly. Emphasise the importance of taking turns and not interrupting each other.

Bury creatures that look similar but have, for example, different numbers of legs. Encourage the children to count the features that they can see and to compare the shapes as they try to guess which animals are hidden. Once the children are confident with the game, let them play in pairs with one child burying an animal and their friend guessing what it might be.

Early Learning Goal
Use everyday words to describe position.

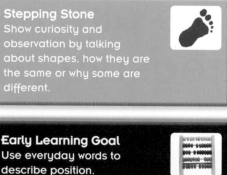

Group size
Up to four children.

What you need
Sand tray; plastic sea animals.

Preparation
Bury some plastic sea animals in the sand, leaving a part of each sticking out.

Support and extension

Prompt younger children with questions about the shape of the creature, size, number of legs and so on to help them guess. Help them to describe it afterwards. Encourage older children to think logically, to develop skills of deduction and to put their thoughts into words. Ask them to describe what they can see and then to explain their reasoning, for example: 'I can see a pointed fin so it must be a fish'; 'I can see a curved shell so it must be a crab'.

Home partnership

Provide a sheet of sea-creature shape 'silhouettes' for the children to take home and share with their families.

Further ideas

♦ Encourage the children to draw pictures of the creatures that they found in the sand, and to write a short sentence underneath explaining why they thought that it was that particular sea creature.
♦ Provide shape sponge printers and make pictures of the sea creatures using different shapes. The children could invent their own weird and wonderful creatures with as many legs as they like!

Theme links
Animals
Opposites
Shapes

The pirate's treasure

Group size
Whole group.

What you need
Neck scarf; piece of 'treasure', such as a necklace or a teddy.

What to do

Talk about pirates with the children. Has anyone ever seen any films or pictures of pirates? What sort of things do pirates say, wear and do? Remind the children that pirates like to search for buried treasure, and explain that you are going to play a game to look for some treasure. Ask the children to sit in a circle on the floor. Explain that when the pirates have found their buried treasure, they guard it very carefully, so if you are going to try to take it from them you will have to move very quietly.

Place your item of treasure in the centre of the circle. Ask an adult or a confident child to take the part of the pirate and sit in the centre of the circle with their eyes closed, guarding the treasure. If they are happy to do so, loosely tie a scarf over their eyes so that they cannot peep.

Point silently to one child sitting in the circle. This child should creep forward very quietly and try to take the treasure. If the pirate hears someone trying to steal the treasure, they should point in the direction that they think they hear the child coming from. If they are correct, they keep the treasure and another child tries to creep up and take it. Once a child manages to reach the treasure it is their turn to be the pirate.

Support and extension

Support younger children by providing an adult to hold their hand and creep with them as they try to take the treasure. With older children, use a bead necklace as treasure, so that it is more likely to make a noise when they try to take it.

Home partnership

Encourage children to play sea-creature guessing games at home. Ask them to pretend to be different sea creatures for the rest of their families to guess.

Further ideas

♦ Play your own seaside versions of 'Grandmother's footsteps' and 'Musical statues', perhaps pretending to be crabs trying to get back to the sea, or pieces of floating seaweed.
♦ Move in contrasting ways pretending to be little or big sea creatures. Remember to include creatures that you would find on the sand as well as in the water.

Theme links
Movement
Sounds

One by one

Stepping Stone
Manipulate materials to achieve a planned effect.

Early Learning Goal
Handle tools, objects, construction and malleable materials safely and with increasing control.

Group size
Two to four children.

What you need
Plastic tongs; a collection of different-sized spoons; pair of chopsticks; treasure chest or box; small toys and treasures, such as plastic and fabric sea creatures; a string of beads; bangles.

Preparation
Place the treasure chest on the floor with the toys or items of treasure spilled around it. Place the tongs and spoons nearby.

What to do
Talk to the children about digging for treasure on the beach. Has anyone ever dug up some pretty shells or perhaps a coin? Show the children the treasure chest and admire together the beautiful treasure that you can see around it. Explain that someone has spilled the treasure out of the chest and you would like the children to help you to pick it up and put it back. But instead of using their fingers, they can only pick up the treasure using the tongs or spoons.

Ask the children if they think they could do this. Talk about which items they think will be easier to pick up with the tongs or spoons. What would be best to use to pick up the small sea creatures? Why? Demonstrate how to use the tools to pick up pieces of treasure, then invite one child to have a go. Go around the group, letting each child try to pick up one piece of treasure, and counting the items as they drop them into the chest. Suggest that they try both the spoons and the tongs each time to see which they find easier. Talk about the textures of the different items. Is it easier to pick up the smooth, slippery items or the soft, fabric ones?

Support and extension
Use a number spinner or large dice and ask younger children to pick up a given number of items. For older children set a time limit using a sand-timer, turning the game into a competition between the players.

Home partnership
Develop these ideas for a seaside fun day. Ask parents and helpers to help supervise a collection of seaside activities aimed at developing the children's manual dexterity.

Further ideas
♦ Play the game outside on a sunny day, trying to pick up larger plastic sea creatures and drop them into a water tray or paddling pool.
♦ Provide lots of different materials for the children to use to build and sculpt their own sea creatures and plants.

Theme links
How things work
Materials
The senses

Treasure trail

Group size
Up to six children.

What you need
Chalk or a length of string; safe, open outdoor area (not grassy); picture of a coastal footpath; obstacles to climb over and through, such as tables, tunnels, benches, mats and staging blocks.

Preparation
Draw a long, windy chalk line on the floor outside, weaving in and out of obstacles. Alternatively, use string to create a trail for the children to walk along.

What to do

Begin by looking at a picture of a coastal footpath with the children. Talk about the cliffs and the sea below. Explain that people like to walk there because the view is so beautiful, but they have to be careful because it can be very dangerous.

Now show the children the trail that you have set up. Ask them to imagine that it is a narrow cliff path, and the obstacles are rocks and tunnels. Tell them that you are all going to walk along the path in single file, placing one foot in front of the other and keeping to the line, so that you do not fall off into the crashing waves below. Explain that at the end of the path there is some treasure and if they are very careful they might reach it.

Lead the children along the trail balancing with one foot carefully in front of the other. Tell them to be sure to leave a space between themselves and the child in front, putting their arms out to help balance but not touching anyone else. As you walk along pretend that the wind is blowing and making you wobble, that the path is overgrown with brambles that you have to step over and the waves are crashing against the rocks showering you with sea spray. When you get to the end of the line, show your relief at arriving safely and gather up some imaginary treasure. Share the treasure out and decide whether to go back along the path or to go home another way.

Support and extension

Make a map for younger children, to add to the fun and develop their role-play ideas. Older children could set out their own cliff-top trail, positioning the obstacles where they want them. Add some blue fabric to represent the sea.

Home partnership

Ask parents to let their children bring in photographs of exciting seaside walks that they have shared. Make a wall display, with captions for each child's photographs.

Further ideas

♦ Discuss safety at the seaside and talk about the dangers as well as the beauty of the scenery.
♦ Think about people that we might need to call on for help if we got stuck on a cliff-top trail. Talk about the lifeguard service and helicopter rescues.

Theme links
Journeys
People who help us
Places around us
Safety

Chapter 4

On the sea

This chapter looks at the activity that goes on above the waves, with ideas to explore all types of boats from tiny sailing vessels to vast pirate ships! Enjoy finding out how cars are ferried across the sea, exploring floating and sinking, and making your very own rocking boats.

All aboard!

Group size
Up to four children.

What you need
20 or more toy cars; a dice with spots or numbers from 1 to 6; cardboard box; ruler; black felt-tipped pen.

Preparation
Make a simple car ferry from a cardboard box with the sides cut down. Cut the front flap so that it can be folded down to let cars on and off. Mark on a parking grid with spaces for 20 toy cars.

What to do
Ask the children if they have ever been on a car ferry. Explain that ferries take people and vehicles across the water. The people drive their cars down to the edge of the water and then on to the ferry. They drive off the ferry when they reach the other side of the river or sea. Show the children the car ferry that you have made and position it on a suitable area of floor space. Ask the children to help you count out up to 20 cars and line them up to wait for the ferry to arrive. Invite one of the children to bring the ferry across the sea and line it up next to the cars.

Ask the children to count the spaces on the ferry and the number of cars waiting. See if they can tell you whether there is enough room for all the cars to park on the ferry. Encourage one child to throw a dice and count that number of cars out of the line and on to the ferry, parking each in a marked space. Ask the child how many cars are parked on the ferry and how many spaces are left.

Now invite the next child to throw the dice and drive more cars on to the ferry. When the ferry is full, sail it across the 'sea', and let the children drive the cars off at the other side.

Stepping Stone
Use some number names accurately in play.

Early Learning Goal
Recognise numerals 1 to 9.

Support and extension
For younger children use only ten cars and a dice with spots or numbers from 1 to 3. Ask older children more complicated mathematical questions involving addition and subtraction.

Home partnership
Ask parents to play counting games with their children at bathtime, sailing different numbers of people across the 'sea' in various containers.

Further ideas
♦ Use toy coaches, instead of cars, and explain that they each take up two spaces on the ferry.
♦ Play the ferry game with play people, eager to get across the sea to the beach on the other side!

Theme Links
Journeys
Size
Transport

Foundation Themes
The Seaside

Pirate Pete

Group size
Whole group.

What you need
Drawing paper; pencils; crayons; whiteboard or flip chart; marker pen.

Preparation
Prepare an area where the children have space to draw and write. Put out a piece of paper for each child and pencils and crayons to share.

What to do
Gather the children around you where they can sit comfortably and listen. Talk to them about some of their favourite stories and introduce the idea of the main character. Explain that you are going to work together to create a character, to build up a picture of him and tell some stories about him. Tell the children that the character's name is Pirate Pete. Does anyone know what a pirate is? Talk about films, books or pictures you have seen and remind the children about the types of clothes that pirates wear. Tell the children that you would like them to help you to draw him, and explain that you will need some help with ideas.

Draw the shape of the pirate's head on to a whiteboard or flip chart. Ask the children to suggest what colour his hair should be, whether he should have a beard, a patch on one eye and so on. Gradually build up the picture, bringing in suggestions from as many children as possible. When the picture is complete ask the children whether they think he was a good or a bad pirate. Talk about the things that he did and whether he was happy or sad. Tell a story about Pirate Pete on his ship, encouraging the children to join in.

Now ask the children to draw their own pictures of Pirate Pete. Talk to each child about their picture and encourage them to tell you a story about their pirate. Acting as scribe, write the stories down. At the end of the session gather the children together, show them the pictures that they drew and read out their stories.

Support and extension
Younger children may need an adult to help them draw their pictures and tell their stories. Older children can try writing their own story about Pirate Pete using a list of useful words.

Theme links
Clothes
Fairy-tales

Home partnership
Make a book of all the children's pictures and stories and put it on display for the parents and carers to come and look at.

Further idea
♦ Encourage the children to use their imagination and to express and communicate ideas by creating other seaside characters, such as a mermaid, a magical fish or a shy octopus. Try telling stories in small groups.

Hats, maps and telescopes

Group size
Up to six children.

What you need
A collection of junk materials and collage items; cardboard tubes; small boxes; silver paper; tape; glue; paper; scissors; soft-toy parrot or bird.

Preparation
Set up a table with junk materials, glue, scissors and tape. Find a suitable story about pirates, perhaps one written by the children as suggested in 'Pirate Pete' on page 50.

What to do
Begin by talking about pirates with the children. Ask them to recall the sort of things that a pirate might wear and carry. Talk about pirate ships and the exciting life that pirates live on the ocean. Tell the children a story about a pirate, introducing the pirate's telescope, map and compass. Ask the children why a pirate would need these things.

Explain that you are going to have some fun pretending to be pirates. What things could you make to help you look the part? Provide a few suggestions to prompt the children, then help them to develop their ideas by showing them how they could use the available junk materials to make some props. Let the children choose freely from the selection, providing help when necessary. Work together to make pirate hats, telescopes, treasure maps and eyepatches, then have fun pretending to be pirates in your role-play area. Do not forget to include a parrot, taped on to your shoulder!

Support and extension
Interact positively with younger children to help keep their play along the right tracks and to develop their imagination and vocabulary. Join in with older children asking who is captain, where they are going and whether anyone has sighted land through their telescope. Suggest that they lower the anchor and take the rowing boat ashore to look for treasure.

Home partnership
Ask the children to bring in books about pirates, treasure islands and ships to share with the group.

Further idea
♦ Arrange your role-play area to look like a desert island or undersea cave.
♦ Make pirate ships from large cardboard boxes decorated with silver foil.

Theme links
Clothes
Favourite stories
Transport

Calming the storm

Stepping Stone
Gain an awareness of the cultures and beliefs of others.

Early Learning Goal
Begin to know about their own cultures and beliefs and those of other people.

Group size
Whole group.

What you need
The bible story 'Jesus Calms the Storm', taken from Bible Stories for the Very Young by Sally Grindley and Jan Barger (Bloomsbury Children's Books); the 'Stormy seas' photocopiable sheet on page 94; scissors; glue sticks; white paper.

Preparation
Make one photocopy of the 'Stormy seas' sheet for each child, plus one extra. Mount the extra sheet on card and cut out the individual pictures.

What to do
Tell the children that you are going to read them a very special story about something that happened at sea. Explain that the story is taken from the Bible. Can anyone tell you what the Bible is? Explain that it is a holy book which tells us all about the life of Jesus. Talk about other holy books, inviting the children to share their own experiences with the group. Talk about the church and other places of worship of relevance to the children in your group. Make sure everyone is included in the discussion and has an opportunity to share their experiences.

Now read the story of Jesus calming the storm. When you have finished reading, talk about the story together. Ask the children to try to imagine how the people in the story would have felt when the sea was rough and the boat was rocking, and then when it was calm. Retell the story using the set of sequencing pictures. Go over each picture carefully in turn, making sure the children are clear about the order of events.

Give each child a photocopied sheet and invite them to cut out and stick the pictures in the correct order on to a sheet of paper. Then ask them to retell the story in their own words.

Support and extension
Give younger children extra adult help with the cutting and sequencing. Suggest that older children write a sentence to go under each picture.

Home partnership
Encourage the children to bring in relevant stories from a variety of cultures and share them with the group.

Further ideas
◆ Act out the story of Jesus calming the storm.
◆ Sing the song 'Here are some boats' on the photocopiable sheet on page 87.
◆ Compare the story with stories from other religions and cultures.

Theme links
Places of worship
Stories from around the world

Rocking boats

Group size
Up to six children.

What you need
Large paper plates; scissors; ruler; tissue paper in shades of blue; glitter; sequins; felt-tipped pens; pencils; PVA glue; white and coloured card; stapler (adult use); pictures of different types of boats, including sailing-boats.

Preparation
Cut out triangles from white card to make the base of the boat and the main sail. Make a sample rocking boat (see illustration).

What to do
Talk about boats with the children. Look at pictures of lots of different boats and name the different parts that you can see. Think about the motion of the boats on the water. Can anyone suggest why boats rock backwards and forwards on the water? Show the children the rocking boat that you have made and ask them if they can think what you used to make it. Show them how it rocks backwards and forwards, just like a sailing boat on the choppy sea.

Invite the children to make a rocking boat to take home. Give each child a paper plate and invite them to use the available materials to decorate it to look like the sea. Fold each plate in half so that they rock when they are stood up, and cut a slit in the top of each one. Explain to the children that you are going to slot the sailing boat into this slit.

Show the children how to tape two triangles together to make the boat and main sail, then let them have fun decorating their boat and sail using their choice of colouring materials, glitter and sequins. Encourage them to add their name somewhere on the boat or the sail. When everyone is happy with their designs, show the children how to poke the bottom of their boat through the slit in the top of their plate, so that the boat looks as if it is sitting on the water. Tape the boats in position so that they stand up. Staple each child's plate 1cm from the top on either side of the boat so that the model rocks but does not open out.

Invite the children to imagine that they are sailing their boats across the sea, and encourage them to tell you where they are sailing to. Display your colourful rocking boats on a table top covered with silver foil or blue paper.

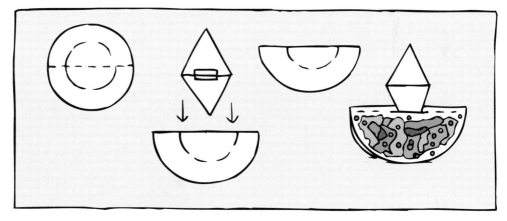

Support and extension
Help younger children with the folding and sticking. Older children could add fishermen and fish to their models.

Home partnership
Ask parents and carers to let their children bring in toy boats from home for a table-top display at your setting. Arrange the boats into sets using different criteria.

Further ideas
♦ Compare and contrast pictures of different parts of boats. Find out how sailing-boats, rowing boats and powerboats move.
♦ Make a display showing vehicles that travel on and under the water. Include lots of different types of boats, ships and submarines.

Theme links
Movement
Shapes
Transport

Row, row, row your boat

Group size
Whole group.

What you need
A large, open floor space.

Preparation
Ask the children to remove their socks and shoes and any excess layers of clothing, so that they are comfortable and can move freely.

What to do

Encourage the children to find a space and sit down with their legs stretched out in front of them. Ask if anyone has ever seen a rowing boat or a rowing machine. Can any of the children demonstrate a rowing movement? Pretend to row together, demonstrating how to hold the imaginary oars, stretch forward and move your arms backwards and forwards while keeping your legs straight on the floor. Once the children have mastered this, ask them to find a partner and sit on the floor facing each other with the soles of their feet touching their partner's.

Sing the song 'Row, Row, Row Your Boat' (Traditional). As you sing, hold hands with your partner and sway backwards and forwards. Now ask the children to imagine they are in a sailing-boat. Sitting in the same position show them how to pull and raise the sail, hand over hand while singing, 'Sail, Sail, Sail your boat'. Try steering the wheel of a pirate ship or paddling a kayak. Praise the children for their ability to listen attentively and follow instructions.

Support and extension

Arrange the pairs of children so that an older, more co-ordinated child works with one who is younger and less confident. Alternatively, provide adult support for younger children who find the activity particularly difficult. For older children, alter the pace of the activity. Start by rowing the boat gently then increase the speed, moving faster. Finish by slowing right down and stopping.

Home partnership

Ask parents' permission to take photographs of the children playing the rowing boat game. Create a display in the entrance to your setting celebrating how well your group play together.

Further ideas

♦ Provide other activities where children can work in pairs and support each other, such as working together to produce a picture of the sea.
♦ Sing other songs about boats and the sea, such as 'Bobby Shaftoe' or 'A Sailor Went to Sea, Sea, Sea' (both Traditional).

Theme links
Nursery rhymes
People who help us

Build a boat

Group size
Up to six children.

What you need
Large cardboard boxes; stacking boxes or large wooden blocks; large, open floor space; musical instruments (optional); dressing-up clothes (optional).

What to do

Remind the children about the different types of boats you have been finding out about. Talk about the similarities and differences between them, and name the various parts of some of the more familiar ones, such as sails, oars, funnels and so on. Ask the children if they would like to help you build a boat in your setting. Count up the number of children in the group and explain that the boat needs to be big enough for all of you to sit in. Look around the room and suggest some suitable items that you could build the boat from; these could be chairs and other safe and practical items, such as storage boxes and large building bricks.

Help the children to gather the items together, and work as a group to make your boat. As you build it, keep checking that the whole of your little group will fit into it. Encourage the children to tell you what sort of boat they are making and where they are going to sail in it.

When you have finished, sit in the boat with the children and use it as a base to tell stories and sing songs from. Bring along some musical instruments to make the sounds of the sea. Add to the role-play experiences by dressing up as pirates, using the clothes and accessories that you made in the 'Hats, maps and telescopes' activity on page 51.

Support and extension

Provide adult support to ensure that younger children are fully involved. Help with lifting and carrying. Suggest that older children design a flag and write a name for the ship on a piece of card.

Home partnership

Encourage parents to let their children turn the dining-room furniture or clothes horse into pirate ships at home!

Further ideas

♦ Make other role-play vehicles to take you on day trips to the seaside, or fly you to a distant beach.

♦ Arrange lengths of appropriately-coloured fabric to create a beach next to some sand. Sit on the beach for circle time or story time.

Theme links
Materials
Our friends
Shapes and sizes

Rescue at sea

Group size
Up to six children.

What you need
Five plastic boats; 15 play people that will fit inside the boats.

What to do
Ask the children to join you, sitting on the floor in a circle. Pretend that the floor in front of you is the sea. Take the five toy boats and place them in the middle of the circle in a line. Provide some play people and ask the children how many people they would like to put in each boat. Talk the children through this and see if they can tell you about the people they are putting into their boats and where they might be sailing to. Are they going on holiday? Perhaps the boats are ferries, taking the play people across the sea?

Pretend that a storm has blown in and begun to tip the boats up, spilling all the people out into the sea. Explain that the sea is cold and rough, the wind is blowing and the sun has gone behind a cloud. Luckily the people are wearing life jackets and float around on top of the waves. Introduce the word 'capsized' and explain that it means to over turn a boat.

Ask the children to imagine how the people might be feeling. Encourage them to talk to you as they play, extending their vocabulary and checking their understanding of less familiar words. Encourage the children to right the boats and rescue the play people that fell into the sea. All through the activity, ask the children how the people would be feeling. Remind them that the people would be cold, wet and frightened and would want to return to the shore to warm up and change into dry clothes.

Ask the children to share any experiences they might have had where they have ended up wet and cold or have felt a bit frightened.

Support and extension
Let younger children play freely moving the people in and out of the boats. Ask an adult to join in the game and help to make up stories about the people in the boats. Encourage older children to tell the story themselves, helping them by extending their vocabulary.

Home partnership
Ask parents and carers for boxes and cartons for the children to build junk sailing-boats with, then invite them to come and see the children's models.

Further ideas
♦ Say the rhyme 'Five coloured boats near a stormy shore' on the photocopiable sheet on page 84.
♦ Broaden the scope of the activity by adding sea creatures to the water. The play people could have encounters with dolphins or perhaps see a mermaid!

Theme links
Journeys
Safety
Transport

Sink or swim

Early Learning Goal
In practical activities and discussion begin to use the vocabulary involved in adding and subtracting.

Group size
Two or three children.

What you need
A story-book, such as Who Sank the Boat? by Pamela Allen (Puffin); plastic toy boats that will float; marbles; bricks such as Multilink; water tray or paddling pool.

Preparation
Set up the water tray with the boats and other items on a table close by.

What to do
Sit the children down comfortably and read them a story about boats. When you have finished reading, discuss the story. Explain that when a boat sits on top of the water we say it is floating but if it drops down under the water we say it is sinking.

Let each child choose a plastic boat and invite them over to the water tray. Talk about the boats that they have chosen and ask them to guess what will happen when they put them on the water. Watch the boats float on the surface of the water, then explain that you are going to try to sink them. Give each child a marble and ask them to place it carefully in their boat. What happens? Can they guess how many marbles their boat will hold before it gets too heavy and sinks? Let the children place a second marble in the boats, again observing and talking about what happens. Continue adding marbles to the boats, counting them as you put them in and watching the boats drop lower in the water and eventually sink as the weight inside them increases. Were the children correct in their guesses about the number of marbles their boats would hold?

Try the same activity with small plastic bricks and compare the results. Remove the cubes and marbles and let the children continue experimenting with plastic sea animals and play people, finding out how many their boats will hold.

Support and extension
Give younger children steady boats that do not tip too easily. Older children could record the results using tally marks to keep track of each item they put into their boat.

Home partnership
Encourage parents to provide their children with simple floating and sinking toys that can be used at home in the bath, sink or paddling pool.

Further ideas
♦ Make simple boats made out of plastic, card and foil containers. Try floating them on the water tray to find which materials make the best boat.
♦ Take photographs of the boats with different numbers of marbles in and arrange them on the wall in order. Write captions to explain why each successive boat sinks lower in the water.

Theme links
How things work
Materials

Making waves

Stepping Stone
Experimant with different ways of moving

Early Learning Goal
Move with confidence, imagination and in safety.

Group size
Up to eight children.

What you need
Lengths of dowel rod (approximately 30cm); lengths of ribbon; CD player or tape recorder; CD or tape of sea music, such as The Hebrides, 'Fingal's Cave' by Mendelssohn; safe, open space; video of crashing waves; video player.

Preparation
Make one ribbon stick for each child by attaching a length of ribbon to a dowel rod. Set up the music-playing facilities.

What to do

Sit the children in a circle in a hall or other large space and show them the video clip of crashing waves.

Talk about the movement of the water. Is it calm? What sort of noises can they hear? Make whooshing noises together and invite the children to join you as you make wave patterns in the air with your hands. Move your hands up and down in front of you like waves on the sea. Now pick up a ribbon stick and show them how to wave it in a similar way to make wave shapes in the air.

Ask the children to stand up and choose a ribbon stick each. Start the music and invite them to join you as you stand on the spot and make waves in the air with your ribbon stick.

Once they have mastered the technique begin to move out of the circle and dance around the room making waves with your ribbons. Wave the ribbons up and down in an undulating movement then round and round in circles.

Turn the music down and gradually slow down, swirling the ribbon in a circle down to the floor and sinking down with it. When everyone is still turn the music very low, place the ribbons on the floor and finish off with the hand movements you started with.

Support and extension

Provide adult support to help younger children with the ribbon sticks. Encourage older children to twist and swirl their bodies to the music as they dance.

Home partnership

Make up a movement sequence to the sea music and invite parents in to watch it.

Further ideas

♦ Use finger-paint and sponge rollers to make big and small waves on sugar paper.
♦ Use a drawing program on the computer to make wave patterns.

Theme links
Movement
Patterns
Shapes

Chapter 5

Under the sea

Take to the open waves with the ideas in this chapter, and encourage children to think about the creatures and plants that live under the water in our vast oceans. Activities include pretending to be seaweed moving in the ocean current, making your own octopus puppets and focusing on the patterns and shapes on fish.

Group size
Up to eight children.

What you need
Lengths of green Cellophane; crêpe paper or bubble wrap; green finger-paint; painting paper; bowl of soapy water; towel; CD or tape of sea music, such as La Mer by Debussy; facilities to play music; table with wipe-clean surface.

Preparation
Cut lengths of green Cellophane, crêpe paper or bubble wrap to represent seaweed. Prepare a table for finger-painting and an area for washing hands.

Swaying seaweed

What to do
Invite the children to join you in a circle with the seaweed lengths in the middle. Ask them if they have ever seen, touched and smelled seaweed. If they have, ask them to help you describe it. Explain that seaweed grows under the sea, attaching itself to rocks and stones and even old shipwrecks on the seabed. The seaweed grows upwards and sways and waves in the water in the same way that plants on land move in the wind.

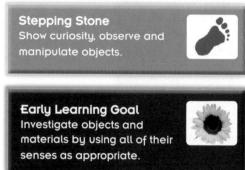

Stepping Stone
Show curiosity, observe and manipulate objects.

Early Learning Goal
Investigate objects and materials by using all of their senses as appropriate.

Encourage the children to choose a length of seaweed to hold. Put on some gentle music and show them how to move their weed, as if it is swaying under the sea. Lift your arm up and down and round in circles and watch to see how the seaweed responds. Recite a simple rhyme to help the children concentrate and focus on what they are doing:

Seaweed waving, Seaweed swaying, Seaweed washing, To and fro.

Repeat the rhyme a couple of times, then ask the children to toss their weed back into the centre of the circle. Explain that seaweed comes loose under the sea and gets washed ashore by the waves.   Take the children over to the painting table and pour some green finger-paint on the table top. Take turns to feel the slippery paint and spread your fingers through it, imagining it is wet seaweed. Encourage the children to use their fingers to draw seaweed shapes in the paint. Take prints by gently pressing paper on top of the paint. Provide a bowl of soapy water for the children to wash in and continue to experience slippery textures.

Support and extension
Ask adult helpers to work with younger children, encouraging them to focus on the movements. Older children could make up a seaweed dance.

Home partnership
Invite parents and carers to watch a dance and movement session.

Further idea
♦ Hang up the lengths of 'seaweed' as part of an undersea display and watch them move in the breeze.

Theme links
Changes
Opposites

Fishy prints

Group size
Up to five children.

What you need
One or more whole fresh fish with large flat scales if possible; pictures of fish, fishing boats, fishermen and nets; newspaper; powder paint; absorbent paper; paintbrushes; bowl of soapy water.

Preparation
Wash and dry the fish, patting the scales with absorbent paper. Make sure they have been cleaned out but are untouched on the surface so that the children can look at, touch and smell the fresh fish. Cover a painting table with newspaper, place the fish in the centre and have the pots of paint ready.

What to do

Sit the children around the table and show them the fish. Explain that, just a short time ago, the fish on the table would have been swimming in the sea. Can anyone explain how the fish got to the supermarket? Share the pictures of the fishing boats and fishermen, and explain how the fish is caught and delivered to the supermarket. Name the parts of the fish; the mouth, eyes, fins, tail and scales. Watch the colours of the scales change in the light and let the children feel and smell the fish. Ask them if they like to eat fish. Maybe they like fish fingers instead of whole fish.

Tell the children that you are going to take a print of the fish. Encourage them to paint the top of the fish with one or two colours of paint, then smooth and press a piece of absorbent paper gently all over to make a complete print. The first print is not always as good as successive ones because there may be too much paint, so take several prints and compare them.

Look at the patterns of the scales on your print and compare them with the original. Ask the children to tell you what they can see. Explain that fresh fish can be bought near the seaside where it is caught as well as at the supermarket, and often tastes especially good.

Support and extension

Ask younger children to point out the eyes, tail, fins and scales on the fish. Older children can write some labels to go with the fish prints. Provide help with the spelling of suitable words.

Home partnership

Ask parents to save the packaging from fish products that they buy at the supermarket. Let the children bring them in to use for a table-top display.

Further ideas

♦ Cut the dry fish prints into fish shapes and stick them on the wall on a background of waves to make a display.
♦ Print some waves on a length of paper with sponges or combs dipped in paint.
♦ Read information books about fishing boats.

Theme links
Colours
Food
Patterns
Shapes

Foundation Themes
The Seaside

My mermaid friend

Group size
Up to 12 children.

What you need
A story about a mermaid, such as *Can You Catch a Mermaid?* by Jane Ray (Orchard Books) or *The Little Mermaid and Other Fairytales* by Hans Christian Andersen (Penguin); small, decorative hand mirror.

Preparation
Arrange a circle of chairs, one for each member of the group.

Stepping Stone
Show care and concern for others, for living things and the environment.

Early Learning Goal
Understand what is right, what is wrong, and why.

What to do

Read or tell the children a story about a mermaid. Explain that mermaids are fairy-tale creatures that live in an undersea world. Instead of legs, mermaids have tails just like a fish. Mermaids can change their tails into legs and walk on the land as long as they bring something from their home under the sea, and keep it with them when they are on land. This could be a necklace, a hairbrush or a special shell.

Tell the children a short story about a mermaid. Ask them to imagine that they meet a mermaid on the beach and become special friends. Everyday the mermaid returns to play with them and tells them all about her home under the sea. She carries a small, decorated hand mirror, which she keeps in her pocket. One day the mirror goes missing. The mermaid cannot return to her home under the sea and is very unhappy. The little girl finds the mirror but knows that if she keeps it the mermaid will stay with her forever. The little girl has to decide whether to do the right thing and return the mirror so that everything can end happily.

Discuss the story, concentrating on the issues of right and wrong. Ask the children if it would be right to keep the mirror, knowing that it belonged to the mermaid. Produce the decorative hand mirror and pass it carefully to one of the children to hold. Ask the children if they can imagine and explain how it would feel to find and hold a mermaid's mirror. Explain to the children that if they would like a turn to speak they must wait until they are holding the mirror. Give each child a turn to speak or to pass the mirror on without contributing if they choose to.

Support and extension

Ask questions to prompt younger children as they hold the mirror. Give older children other imaginary situations and ask them to decide what would be the right thing to do.

Home partnership

Share children's successes and good deeds by praising them in front of their parents and carers and reinforcing their positive behaviour.

Further ideas

♦ Draw a mermaid on an undersea background on the wall. Put individual scales cut from shiny paper in a basket next to the display. When children are kind or helpful, let them stick a scale with their name on it on to the mermaid's tail.
♦ Share the rhyme 'A mermaid sings' on the photocopiable sheet on page 85.

Theme links
Friends
People who help us

Fancy fish

Group size
Up to five children.

What you need
Paper plates; children's scissors; PVA glue; sticky tape; coloured and shiny paper; sequins; fabric scraps; stapler (adult use).

Preparation
Draw a triangle on each paper plate, from the centre out to the edge. Cut the coloured paper into triangles and circles a little bigger than a two-pence piece. Make a sample fish for demonstration purposes (see illustration).

What to do

Show the children the fish that you have made and ask them if they can guess what it is made of. Give each child a paper plate and, using clear and simple instructions, show the children how to cut along the lines on their plate to make a large triangular mouth. Encourage them to tape the triangle at the other end of their fish to make a tail. Go around the group helping with the cutting if necessary and stapling the tails in place.

Provide the children with an assortment of coloured circles and triangles to make scales to decorate their fish. Encourage them to work independently, and to talk about how they aim to decorate their fish, discussing the shapes and colours they plan to use.

Invite the children to take turns to show their fish to the group and to tell the others about the decorations they have chosen. When everyone has had a turn, invite the children to hold up their fish and weave them about in the air as if they were swimming. Talk about the way that real fish move in water, using their tails and fins to help them glide silently along.

Support and extension

Provide younger children with extra help to cut and stick. Encourage a group of older children to make their fish, then sit next to a child in another group and explain what to do.

Home partnership

Ask the children if they have fish at home in a tank, bowl or pond. Perhaps parents could take them to a pet shop or local pond to watch the fish.

Further ideas

◆ Turn the fish into mobiles by suspending them from thread. Position them in a draft so that they 'swim' around.
◆ Organise a visit to an aquarium, where you can watch lots of different fish swimming.
◆ Sing the song 'Swimming fish' on the photocopiable sheet on page 88.

Theme links
Materials
Movement

Foundation Themes
The Seaside

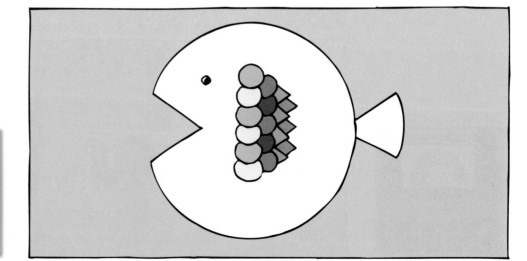

Create a sea creature

Stepping Stone
Begin to describe the texture of things.

Early Learning Goal
Explore colour, texture, shape, form and space in two or three dimensions.

Group size
Up to eight children.

What you need
Clay; rolling-pins; plastic knives; clay tools; pencils; paint; PVA glue; brushes; plastic fish-shaped cutters (optional); models of sea creatures.

Preparation
Cut a lump of clay for each child. Prepare a sink of soapy water for the children to wash their hands in.

What to do

Give the children a lump of damp clay each and let them explore its texture and plasticity. Explain that clay is dug up from the ground and contains a lot of water. Show them the bag that it is kept in and explain that the bag needs to be kept tightly closed to keep the moisture in and prevent the clay from drying out and becoming hard. Look at some sea-creature models together and talk about the different materials that they are made from. Explain that you are going to use the clay to make your own models.

Ask the children to roll their piece of clay into a ball in their hands so that the surface becomes smooth. Encourage them to roll it flat on the table with a rolling-pin and then draw a fish shape on to the surface with a pencil. Make sure the clay is not rolled too thinly or it will break when it hardens.

Show the children how to use the end of the pencil to make scale marks and other patterns in the clay. Help them to cut out their fish shapes with a strong plastic knife. As well as fish, try making other creatures, such as an octopus from a ball of clay and eight sausage-shaped legs or a crab, with a flatter body and shorter legs.

As the children work, discuss the changes that take place. Notice that the clay has become harder and may have changed colour a little. Why might this be? When the sea creatures are dry, let the children paint and then varnish them with watered down PVA glue. Display them on a sea of blue tissue paper.

Support and extension

Provide younger children with adult support for the rolling and cutting stages. Give older children extra clay to try making sea monsters or mermaids.

Home partnership

Wrap the children's models carefully in tissue paper and label with the child's name. Let them take the models home as a gift for a family member.

Further idea

♦ Make tiles from squares of clay and use a variety of tools to produce different wave and sea-creature patterns in the surface.

Theme links
Change
Materials
The senses

Ollie the octopus

Stepping Stone
Initiate interactions with other people.

Early Learning Goal
Have a developing awareness of their own needs, views and feelings and be sensitive to the needs, views and feelings of others.

Group size
Two to four children.

What you need
Three paper plates per puppet; stapler (adult use); pens; collage materials; felt-tipped pens.

Preparation
To make the puppets take two paper plates – one for the top and one for the bottom of the octopus. Fold a third plate in half and staple in place between the other two plates to make the mouth. Cut eight legs from fabric or thin card and staple them to the body. Leave the back of the octopus unstapled so that you can put your hand in to open and close the mouth (see illustration).

What to do
Talk about sea creatures with the children. Have a brainstorming session to see how many different sea creatures you can name. Which sea creature has the most legs? Show the children your octopus puppet and make it 'talk' to the children. Tell them that your name is Ollie and explain that you are lonely and would like to find some other octopuses to talk to. Ask the children if they will help to make some friends for Ollie.

Give each child an octopus puppet, demonstrating how to open and close the mouth to make the puppet talk. Encourage the children to use their own choice of colours and materials to decorate their puppet, giving it well-defined eyes above the mouth. Ask the children to think up a name for their octopus and suggest where it might live.

Let the children play freely in pairs, helping their octopuses to introduce themselves to each other. Tell the children that Ollie is really looking forward to meeting his new friends. Encourage the children to introduce their octopuses to Ollie and to say a little about themselves. Ask the children in the group to speak one at a time and to listen to each other.

Support and extension
Help younger children and encourage them to speak by introducing your puppet to them, talking quietly and pretending to be shy. Encourage older children to speak in detail about the imaginary home of their puppet.

Home partnership
Let the children take their puppets home overnight. Explain that you would like the children to introduce the puppet to their home and family and then bring them back the next day to tell the group about their overnight visit.

Further idea
♦ Set up an undersea world with small-world toys where pairs of children or a child and an adult can play and talk together.

Theme links
Homes
Ourselves

Spotty fish

Stepping Stone
Recognise numerals 1 to 5, then 1 to 9.

Early Learning Goal
Recognise numerals 1 to 9.

Group size
Up to four children.

What you need
The 'Fishy fun' photocopiable sheet on page 95; card; pictures of fish with different patterns and colours.

Preparation
Photocopy the 'Fishy fun' sheet twice on to card. Laminate (if possible), then cut out the individual cards so that you have two sets.

What to do

Begin by looking at the pictures of fish. Notice the different patterns and shapes that you can see. Can you find any fish that look similar or the same? Encourage the children to tell you why the fish look similar. Is it the shapes on the fish, or maybe the colours? See how many fish the children can find with, for example, one spot. Tell the children that you are going to play some games to match up pairs of fish.

Place the spotty fish cards in a pile next to you and spread the numbered fish cards out face down on the table. Ask the children in turn to choose one card and read out the number on it. Let them keep the fish they have chosen, placing it face up on the table in front of them. Now turn over one of the spotty fish and hold it up. The children must count the spots on the card and see if they have the numbered fish to match. If they do, they can take the fish and make a pair.

At the end of the game muddle all the cards up together and place them face up on the table. Ask the children in turns to try to find a pair. Now turn the cards over and ask each child to turn over two cards and see if they make a pair. If not then they must turn them back over, returning them to the same place on the table and trying to remember where they are for later in the game.

Support and extension

Limit the number of cards that you use with younger children, perhaps having just two of each number. For older children, add more cards with numbers up to 10.

Home partnership

Give children a 'Fishy fun' photocopiable sheet to take home. Ask parents to make the cards with their children and play pairing games with them.

Further ideas

♦ Play a game of one more and one less. Place the numbered fish on the table and ask a child to find the fish that is one more than 3 or one less than 5. Count the fish then ask how many there would be if one more swam along to play.

♦ Play matching and pairing games using plastic sea creatures.

Theme links
Numbers
Opposites
Patterns

Red scale, blue scale

Group size
One or two children.

What you need
The 'Fish patterns'
photocopiable
sheet on page 96;
sheets of circular
stickers in three
different colours;
pictures of tropical
fish.

Preparation
Make four copies of
the 'Fish patterns'
photocopiable
sheet.

What to do
Look at some pictures of tropical
fish with the children. Talk about
the vivid colours and the patterns
of spots and stripes that you can see. Have any of the children seen fish like these
before? Perhaps some of them have tropical fish at home. Explain that these fish live
in the sea, where they swim among the bright corals and sea anemones.

Show the children the fish shapes on the photocopiable sheet, and explain that
you are going to make a pattern on the first one. As the children watch, create a
repeating pattern by sticking the coloured stickers across the fish. Keep it simple,
perhaps red, blue, red, blue, or similar. Now ask the children to help you make a
pattern on the second fish, so that both fish look exactly the same. Ask the children
to tell you which colours you have used and what colour you will need next.

Give each child a copy of the 'Fish patterns' sheet. Ask them to make a pattern
on the top one and then swap sheets with a partner and copy the pattern that their
friend has made. Look at the two completed sheets and compare the patterns. Ask
each child to describe the patterns, name the colours they have used and count the
number of spots on their fish.

Support and extension
Give younger children plenty
of practice with physical
objects like pegs and beads
before they try making patterns
with stickers. Challenge older
children by making more
complex patterns for them to
copy, using up to four colours.

Home partnership
Encourage parents and carers
to look for fabric and other
materials with fish and seaside
images at home to bring in to
your setting to make a seaside
patterns display.

Further ideas
♦ Make mirror-image pairs of
fish using blot-pattern painting.
Paint one fish with bright
colours then fold the paper in
half and press down. Open up
the sheet to reveal your mirror-
image fish.
♦ Create a pattern on a blank
fish on the photocopiable sheet
without the children seeing.
Describe it for them to copy on
their own fish. When you have
finished, let the children see
your fish and compare them.

Theme links
Colours
Opposites
Shapes

Treasure sort

Group size
Up to four children.

What you need
A small treasure chest or box with a lid; play treasure, such as necklaces, bangles, beads and coins; card; scissors (adult use); gummed paper shapes; sticky tape.

Preparation
Fill the treasure chest with your play treasure. Cut a card crown or bangle to fit each child.

What to do

Begin by talking about buried treasure with the children. Initiate a discussion about pirates and shipwrecks, and ask the children how pirates know where to look for treasure. Explain that you found a treasure map, and when you dug at the spot marked with a cross, you found a treasure chest packed full of goodies! Invite the children to open the chest and see what's inside. Tell them that the treasure has got muddled up, and you would like them to help you sort it out.

Let the children take turns to choose items of treasure and begin to sort them into sets. Invite them to help you to name the categories and explain why an item does or does not belong to a set. Encourage the children to look carefully at each item and to describe as best they can what it is made of, what shapes and colours they can see in it and so on. Count the items in the sets and ask questions to determine which set has more, less or the same amount.

Once all the treasure has been sorted, give each child a card crown or bangle. Invite them to decorate their jewellery by making a pattern with gummed shapes. Ask the children about the pattern they have made and the shapes and colours that they have used. Show the children how to curve the card to fit their heads or their wrists, then tape the ends securely together. Let the children wear their creations and finish the session with a story about a treasure hunt or sunken treasure under the sea.

Support and extension

For younger children keep the sorting categories simple, making sets of necklaces, coins, beads and bangles. Use sorting hoops with older children. Encourage them to count the items inside each hoop and record the results using tally marks.

Home partnership

Let the children wear their crowns or bangles home. Encourage them to talk about the pattern and colours that they have used.

Further ideas

♦ Thread beads or pasta to make your own treasure.
♦ Roll up strips of paper to make beads. Decorate with paint and glitter and string them together to make necklaces.

Theme links
Clothes
Shapes

Foundation
Themes
The Seaside

Floating jellyfish

Group size
Up to four children.

What you need
Pictures or video clips of jellyfish; paper cups; wool; thin strips of fabric or Cellophane; circles of paper; felt-tipped pens; glue or tape; a sharp pencil; CD or tape recording of calm music, such as Gymnopédie, No. 1 by Satie; CD or cassette player.

Preparation
Make a row of holes around the edge of the cups with a sharp pencil, big enough to thread the fabric or Cellophane through. Cut the fabric or Cellophane into 20cm strips.

What to do
Show the children pictures of real jellyfish or watch a video clip. Notice the jellyfish waving their tentacles and move your fingers in a similar fashion. Invite the children to make their own jellyfish models with waving tentacles.

Give each child a cup and show them how to push the material through the holes. Use glue or tape to secure the ends. Invite the children to give their jellyfish faces by drawing features on to a circle of paper and sticking it on to the side of the cup. Play some calm music and let the children move their jellyfish gently through the air, watching the tentacles swing and sway as they move. Thread a piece of wool through the top of each jellyfish and hang them up where the children can watch the tentacles wave in the air.

Support and extension
For younger children make sure the holes are quite large and provide extra help with threading. Give older children a selection of materials to thread and let them choose their own colour scheme for their jellyfish.

Home partnership
Provide threading fish for the children to take home. Cut fish or starfish shapes from thick card, punch holes around the edges and ask parents to supply their children with string, laces or wool to thread. Strengthen the ends of string or wool by binding the ends with sticky tape.

Further ideas
♦ Attach some lengths of fabric or Cellophane to a piece of string or a belt. Let the children wear their 'tentacle skirts' as they dance and move around gracefully to some gentle music.
♦ If possible, visit an aquarium to watch real jellyfish.

Theme links
Movement
Sounds

Chapter 6

Going on holiday

Encourage children to share their own experiences of day trips and holidays by the sea with the ideas in this chapter. Activities include packing a bag for a trip to the beach, sending postcards to family and friends, and enjoying some seaside-inspired music and movement sessions!

Dressing for the beach

Group size
Whole group.

What you need
Pictures of modern and old-fashioned swimwear; samples of actual swimwear; books about seaside holidays in the past; roll of sugar paper; felt-tipped pens; paints; coloured paper.

Preparation
Set up the books, pictures and samples of swimwear to make a table-top display.

What to do
Talk to the children about times when they have gone swimming at the seaside. Look at the table-top display together and see if the children can tell you what sort of clothing they wear when they go swimming. Now look at the pictures of old-fashioned bathing suits and bathing huts. How do the people and scenery in the pictures compare to the seaside scenes that the children are familiar with today? Look at the differences between the swimming costumes that the children wear today and those worn long ago. Which do the children prefer? Look at and compare each item in turn, for example an old bathing cap with the modern swimming cap and the bathing suit with modern trunks and bikinis.

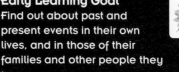

Stepping Stone
Begin to differentiate between past and present.

Early Learning Goal
Find out about past and present events in their own lives, and in those of their families and other people they know.

Ask for two volunteers to be models. Spread some sugar paper on the floor and ask the children to lie carefully on top of the paper. Draw around the children and invite the group to help you to make life-size pictures of a modern and an old-fashioned swimmer. Draw the outlines of the clothing on to coloured paper and cut them out. Ask the children to help you decide which model each item of clothing belongs to, depending on whether it is modern or old fashioned, and let the children stick them in place.

Draw a face on each model and label the items of clothing. Display the pictures along with other pictures and books about the seaside in the past and present.

Support and extension
Help younger children to recall the past by looking at photographs of outings and special occasions. Older children could make a time line, sequencing holiday pictures of themselves from when they were babies to the present day.

Home partnership
Ask parents to contribute labelled and dated seaside items for your collection.

Further idea
♦ Make an old-fashioned Punch and Judy tent. Let the children make some puppets and put on their own seaside puppet show.

Theme links
Changes
Clothes
Growing
Time

Picture postcards

Early Learning Goal
Write their own names and
other things such as labels
and captions and begin
to form simple sentences,
sometimes using punctuation.

Group size
Up to ten children.

What you need
Postcards from
beaches in this
country and around
the world; crayons;
pencils; felt-tipped
pens; one plain
postcard per child;
posters or books
(or even holiday
brochures) with
pictures of tropical
beaches; a box
containing each
child's name written
on a slip of paper;
shoulder bag;
display board.

Preparation
Display the
postcards on
a board at the
children's height.

What to do
Explain that sometimes, when people go away on holiday, they like to send their families and friends postcards that show where they are staying. Show the children the picture postcards, and enjoy working out together where they might have been sent from. Ask the children if they have ever been to a far off country. Perhaps some of them can tell you something about their holiday or visit. Remain sensitive to children who have not travelled, and include their contributions about day trips they have enjoyed. Show the children some posters of tropical beaches, then explain that you are going to pretend that you are all off on holiday, and you are going to make some postcards to send back home.

Give each child a blank postcard. Encourage the children to draw a colourful tropical beach on one side of their postcard. Then let them pick a slip of paper from the box with another child's name on, to send their postcard to. Help each child to copy the name they have picked on the back of their postcard and sign their own name on the bottom.

Place all the cards in a shoulder bag and pretend that the cards are being sent on an aeroplane across the sea. Later on pretend that the post has arrived. Sit the children in a circle and pull out one card at a time from the bag. Call out the name of the child who sent the card and invite them to deliver it the correct child. Let the children take their postcards home.

Support and extension
Younger children could stick pictures cut from holiday brochures on to their postcards. Encourage older children to write a sentence on their postcard.

Home partnership
Ask parents to help their child to learn their home address. Read out the addresses in turn and ask, 'Who lives here?'. Do this regularly and then, when the children are ready, let them recite their own addresses to you.

Further ideas
♦ Ask children to bring in postcards from home. Talk about where they have come from and find the places on a globe or world map.
♦ Tie the activity in to work you have been doing on other countries. Collect postcards, pictures, clothes and samples of food to make an interactive display.

Theme links
Food from around
the world
Our families
Weather

Foundation Themes
The Seaside

What shall we pack?

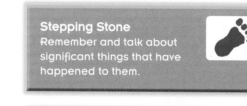
Group size
Up to ten children.

What you need
Suitcase or backpack; carrier bag; collection of clothes – some suitable for a summer beach holiday and some not, including swimwear, T-shirt, shorts, sun-hat, sun-glasses, woolly hat, scarf, gloves and thick jumper; towel; bucket and spade; suncream.

Preparation
Place all the items in the carrier bag.

What to do
Gather the children together in a circle and talk about holidays in the sun. Ask them to think about what they would need to pack in their suitcase if they were going on a holiday to the seaside. Describe an imaginary resort, the sort of weather that you are expecting and the activities that you plan to do. Show them the empty suitcase and ask them to help you decide what to pack.

Tip out a selection of clothes from the carrier bag including some woolly gloves, a warm hat, a swimsuit, T-shirt and shorts. Hold up two contrasting items and ask the children to decide which of the two items you should pack in your suitcase. Ask them to explain the reason for their decisions, then pack the chosen items in the case and put the discarded ones aside.

Explain that it will be hot and sunny some of the time and you will need something to protect you from the sun. See if the children can point out the suncream, sun-glasses and sun-hat.

Continue with buckets and spades and beach toys and something to take for a rainy day. Check to see if there is room for everything in the suitcase or if you have chosen too many things.

Conclude by sharing the children's experiences of holidays and trips that they have been on and events that happened to them, as well as future trips and holidays or outings that the children will be going on soon.

Support and extension
For younger children limit the number of items to be packed. Older children might like to suggest games to pass the time on a long journey.

Home partnership
Ask the children to bring in a favourite holiday snap. Encourage them to tell you about the journey, who went with them and what they did when they arrived.

Further ideas
♦ Provide some child-sized cases to use in the role-play area or pretend you are packing a picnic or a bag for swimming.
♦ Let the children help to dress a doll or teddy in clothing that is suitable for a holiday to the rainforest or a ski resort!
♦ Say the rhyme 'I'm going to the seaside!' on the photocoiable sheet on page 85.

Early Learning Goal
Find out about past and present events in their own lives, and in those of their families and other people they know.

Theme links
Hot and cold
Journeys
Opposites
Transport

Foundation
Themes
The Seaside

Our day trip

Stepping Stone
Show an interest in the world in which they live.

Early Learning Goal
Observe, find out about and identify features in the place they live and the natural world.

Group size
Whole group.

What you need
A backpack; some items of litter, such as an empty juice carton and crisp packet; a large, open space indoors or outside.

What to do

Sit the children together in a circle. Explain that you are going to take an imaginary trip to the seaside, and you would like them to help you to mime your trip. Say: 'We're off to the seaside, let's get ready to go. First we need to pack our backpacks; let's decide what to take. Let's make some sandwiches. What shall we put inside them? Our picnic is ready, what else do you think we will need? Have you all got your sun-hats? Can you fit anything else in? Is it full? Put it on your back, and let's set off. How shall we get there? Shall we take the train? Good idea. What can you see through the train window? Are we nearly there? Can you see the sea yet?'.

Mime the journey and the walk down to the beach. Continue: 'Is your backpack heavy? Let's find a place to sit and eat our picnic. Does that sandwich taste good?'. Encourage the children to join in, asking individuals questions about their journey and the picnic as you go. At the end, pack up all your things and set off on the journey home.

Ask the children if they enjoyed their trip to the seaside, then produce the backpack and tip out the litter. Look at the children with a shocked face and ask them whether they remembered to pick up the litter after the picnic. Talk about the importance of leaving the beach clean and taking any rubbish home or putting it in the bin. Put your litter in the bin and remind the children to do the same.

Support and extension

Provide extra adult support to help younger children mime the actions. Older children could design posters about litter, protection from the sun or caring for the environment.

Home partnership

Provide sun awareness or anti-litter badges for the children to wear home. Discuss them with the children and parents at home time.

Further ideas

♦ Pretend to pack a backpack for other trips, such as a fishing trip or a day at a water park.
♦ Sing the song 'On a sunny day' on the photocopiable sheet on page 88.

Theme links
Our world
Recycling
Safety

Foundation
Themes
The Seaside

Seaside dance

Stepping Stone
Develop a repertoire of actions by putting a sequence of movements together.

Early Learning Goal
Use their imagination in art and design, music, dance, imaginative and role-play and stories.

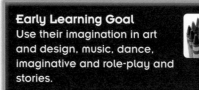

Group size
Up to 10 children.

What you need
A CD or tape of sea music, such as 'Four Sea Interludes' fro Peter Grimes by Britten; CD or cassette player; scarves.

What to do
Invite the children to join you sitting in a circle with your legs stretched out in front of you. Ask everyone to close their eyes and imagine that they are at the seaside. Encourage the children to tell you what they can hear and feel. Explain that you are going to pretend to be at the seaside as you enjoy some movement activities. Begin by pretending that you are sitting on the sand at the beach, dipping your toes in the sea. Demonstrate by pointing your toes and feeling the water trickling over them. Pretend that the water is cold and flex your toes upwards out of the water. Do this several times then kick up and down in the water, still sitting with legs outstretched.

Once you have all warmed up, jump up and squat on your toes in the sand, put your hands in the water and wave them about. Check that everyone is joining in then stand up and stretch towards the sky. Pretend that you can feel the warm sun on your face.

Now put on the music and hand out scarves. Dance around the room to the music, waving the scarves up and down and round and round to create a feeling of the waves in the sea.

At the end of the session collect the scarves and ask the children to lie down in a space on the floor. Play a game of 'Wake the fish'; swim silently in between the children and touch one child on the shoulder, then move to the side of the room. This child should then swim off, wake another sleeping fish and then join you at the side of the room. Continue until all the children are standing quietly with you.

Support and extension
Provide extra adult help to model movements for younger children. Older children could work on simple dance routines in pairs.

Home partnership
Ask parents and carers to play some appropriate music at home for their children to dance to. Encourage the children to choose a sea creature and make up a short routine to share with the other children back at your setting.

Further ideas
♦ Make up a 'Follow-the-Leader' seaside dance routine.
♦ Choose different sea creatures as the focus for your movement sessions. Pretend to be crabs scuttling sideways, manta rays gliding gracefully through the sea or playful dolphins diving in and out of the water.

Theme links
Dance
Movement

Foundation
Themes
The Seaside

Songs of the sea

Stepping Stone
Sing a few simple, familiar songs.

Early Learning Goal
Recognise and explore how sounds can be changed, sing simple songs from memory, recognise repeated sounds and sound patterns and match movements to music.

Group size
Whole group.

What you need
Posters of the seaside; whiteboard or flip chart; marker pen; safe, open space.

Preparation
Put up the posters around your chosen open space, where everyone can see them.

What to do
Sit the children together in a circle. Talk about car journeys that the children have been on. What can we do to help the time pass more quickly on long car journeys? The children may suggest playing 'I spy', looking for different-coloured cars or counting landmarks. Explain that you are going to pretend that you are all on your way to a holiday at the seaside and you are going to sing some songs on your journey. Ask the children to think of some of their favourite songs and sing them together. Explain that you would like some help to make up a special seaside song. Begin by asking them to look at the posters and to tell you what they think of when they see pictures of the seaside. Write down the words they come up and work together to create a simple song.

Using a familiar tune, such as 'Hickory, Dickory, Dock', hum the tune through a couple of times then ask the children to join in, humming and patting their knees to the rhythm. Put together some words for the first verse such as:

> We're going down to the sea,
> The beautiful, beautiful sea.
> The sun is out, the sky is blue,
> We're going down to the sea.

Ask the children if they think they could sing with you. Encourage them to listen to you as you sing the first line through, then repeat it, asking them to join in. Do this with each line then put the whole song together and sing it through a few times.

Make up a second verse together, keeping the first, second and fourth lines the same and adding something different for the third line. This keeps the writing process to a minimum and the repetition makes it easier for the children to learn the tune and the words. For a second verse try, 'The waves are high, the water's cool' or perhaps 'The sand is soft, it tickles my toes'. Ask the children for their ideas and involve them as much as possible in the song-writing process.

Use the finished song to sing as part of a 'going on holiday' role-play incorporating the children's experiences from previous activities.

Support and extension
For younger children, stick to just one verse and encourage them to pat their knees to the rhythm and join in with the words when they feel ready. Older children could have a go at writing several verses. Write each verse down and point to the words as you sing.

Home partnership
Incorporate your seaside songs into a simple concert and invite parents and carers along.

Further ideas
♦ Make some simple costumes from fabric remnants to wear for your seaside song concert.
♦ Organise a day trip to the seaside to enjoy the entertainments and music on offer.

Theme links
Patterns
Songs and rhymes

Foundation
Themes
The Seaside

Circle time

This chapter provides ideas for integrating the theme of 'The seaside' into your circle time sessions. Begin each session by encouraging the children to talk about and share their own experiences of day trips or holidays to the seaside, before moving on to explore your chosen focus.

What you need
A mermaid toy; story about a mermaid, such as Disney's The Little Mermaid (Ladybird).

The mermaid's world

What to do
Begin by reading the mermaid story to the children. Ask them to think about where the mermaid might live. Invite the children to close their eyes and try to imagine the undersea land where the mermaid might swim and play every day.

Make some suggestions, for example: 'The green and purple seaweed waves gently in the warm water, there are coloured shells and coral on the seabed and beautiful fish swim in and out of the weed. The mermaid is sitting in her undersea palace, which is made of pale pink rock decorated with shells.'

Ask the children to open their eyes and to think whether it would be fun to be the mermaid living under the sea. Pass a toy mermaid around the circle and ask the children in turn to say what they think the mermaid would like about living under the sea. For example: 'I think the mermaid would like having a seahorse to ride'; 'I think she would like having the fish to swim with'. Conclude the session by asking the children to think about the things that they would miss about their own life on the land if they lived in the mermaid's undersea world.

Stepping Stone
Express needs and feelings in appropriate ways.

Early Learning Goal
Have a developing awareness of their own needs, views and feelings and be sensitive to the needs, views and feelings of others.

Further ideas
♦ Encourage the children to draw pictures of the mermaid and tell their own stories about her.
♦ Set up an undersea role-play area and enjoy pretending to be mermaids.
♦ Build an undersea world for the mermaid doll and encourage pairs of children to work together to act out the story.

Seaside show and tell

What you need
A collection of seaside items, such as a shell, toy boat, seaside picture, toy fish and fishing net.

What to do

Give the children the option of bringing in an item from home to do with the sea and place the named items on display for a few days. Have a few extra items in case some of the children are not able to bring anything in to the setting.

Make a circle of chairs and invite the children, one at a time, to collect their seaside object, sit down and place their object on the floor in front of them. Explain the importance of sitting quietly and listening to each other, of waiting for a turn to speak and not interrupting each other. Explain also that if they decide not to have a turn they may choose to pass their 'go' on to the next child in the circle.

Start off with an object that you have brought in. Tell the children what it is and where you bought or found it. Give as much information as possible by explaining what the item is used for, whether it once had something living in it, whether it is from the sea or the land and what you use it for now. Ask the children whether they think it is a natural object, or something that somebody has made. Invite each child in turn to show their own seaside item and offer an explanation in their own words. Prompt where necessary, asking the child what they have brought, where they think it came from and why they like it. Respond positively to each child and thank them for bringing in their object and showing it to the group. Give any child who has decided to pass the chance to change their mind and have a turn. Finish the session by grouping the objects according to whether they are natural, manufactured, bought, found and so on. At the end of the session ask each child to return their object to the display table.

Further idea

♦ Sort the items into sets on the display table. Label the sets according to the children's own chosen criteria, for example, what they look like, what they feel like or what they are made of.

Safety at sea

What you need
A hand puppet or soft toy.

What to do

Sit in a circle with the children and introduce your puppet 'Rosie' to the group. Explain that Rosie is going to the beach for the first time and she does not know what to expect. She is a little bit frightened. Pretend that the puppet is whispering her anxieties to you then share her anxieties with the group. Encourage the children to think of ways to reassure Rosie and help her to overcome her fears.

Ask the children to put up their hands if they have been to the beach. Perhaps different children would like to describe what the beach looks like, how the sand feels under foot, what sounds they might hear and so on. See if someone can tell Rosie what the sea smelled like. Was the sea frightening? What could Rosie do if she is frightened of the waves? Perhaps she could hold an adult's hand and they could paddle in the sea and jump the waves together.

Discuss all kinds of fears and anxieties about the sea as well as safety issues. Invite the children in turn to talk about their own experiences or ask them to use their imagination and think about what they would do in a particular situation. Help them out with ideas of your own if they are unsure or have little or no experience of the sea.

As the session progresses explain that Rosie is becoming less anxious, until, by the end of the session, she is excited and looking forward to her trip to the beach. Thank the children for their help and for being so kind to Rosie. Remind them to talk to an adult or an older child if they are worried about anything.

Further idea

♦ Discuss other places that might worry the children, such as a doctor's surgery or starting a new school. Talk about ways that you can help to overcome your fears, for example, by making friends with new people or holding an adult's hand.

King Neptune

What to do

Sit the children in a circle and show them the paper crown. Can anyone suggest who might wear a crown? Would it be a king or a queen? Perhaps they have seen some pictures in fairy-tale books of princes and princesses wearing

What you need
A child-sized paper crown.

Early Learning Goal
Sustain attentive listening, responding to what they have heard by relevant comments, questions or actions.

beautiful crowns. Explain that you are going to play a game; the person who is wearing the crown becomes Neptune, King of the Sea. King Neptune can do magic, turning the rest of the group into whatever he likes, such as fish, crabs, seahorses, mermaids or dolphins.

Put the crown on your head and say, 'I am Neptune, King of the Sea and I turn you into…'. Say the name of your chosen sea creature, and encourage the children to pretend to be that sea creature until you say, 'Stop'. Now ask for a volunteer to be Neptune. Place the crown on that child's head and let them magically change the rest of the group into their chosen sea creature. Make sure all of the children that want to have a turn are given the chance to wear the crown, and that children that do not want to have the opportunity to refuse.

After a few turns take back the crown and explain that Neptune also mixes magic potions for good spells. Encourage the children to suggest a good spell, such as, a picnic to share with everyone, making everyone feel happy or making the sun shine for the whole day. Ask the children what they think you will need to make this potion. Invite them to mime adding their ingredient into a pretend cauldron and mixing it in.

Put on your crown and take on the character of Neptune again. Stir the cauldron together then clap your hands and say some magic words. Invite the children to mime a response to your spell, then again let volunteers take turns to be Neptune.

Further ideas

♦ Use the crown at odd moments to distract children who are unhappy or are being disruptive. Put on the crown and mix up a happy spell to help gain their attention and focus them on something positive.

♦ Make some magic mermaid wands for undersea role-play.

Displays

Displays play a vital part in all early years settings, providing the opportunity to celebrate the achievements of every child in your group. This chapter provides ideas for working together to create four colourful displays that will provide plenty of scope for interaction and conversation.

Starting with 's'

What you need
Display table; tray of seaside items, most beginning with 's'; display board; rolls of bright blue, pale blue and yellow backing paper; 'Seaside shapes' photocopiable sheet on page 89; grey sugar paper; pictures of other seaside items beginning with 's', such as swimmer, stone, seal, sea anemone, sea urchin, sting-ray and speedboat; labels for each picture; Blu-Tack; scissors.

Preparation
Enlarge the 'Seaside shapes' photocopiable sheet to about three times the original size on to grey paper. Cut out the silhouette shapes.

What to do
Cover the display board with yellow paper at the bottom for the sand, blue for the sea and a paler blue for the sky. Label these sections. Cut out the pictures of the seaside items and, if possible, laminate them. Print or write a label for each item and laminate these to.

Using the display
♦ Ask the children if they can think what the labels on the display board might say. Explain that the words 'sky', 'sea' and 'sand' all begin with the same initial sound. Ask them if they can tell you what sound this is. Explain that this is going to be a seaside picture and everything in it will begin with 's'.
♦ One at a time produce the pictures and silhouettes and ask the children to name them and say whether they should go on the sky, sea or sand section. Attach the pictures with Blu-Tack so that they can be moved around and used again at a later date. When all of the pictures have been attached to the display, read out the card labels and invite individual children to match them to the correct pictures.
♦ Now produce the tray of seaside objects and let the children take turns to select and name an item. Ask them to put it on the display table if it begins with 's'. Ask for suggestions of other items that could be added to the display. If the children suggest items that do not begin with 's', explain that they have the wrong initial sound so do not belong on your display. Enjoy returning to the finished display to recap on the names of the objects and to add other seaside items that start with 's'.

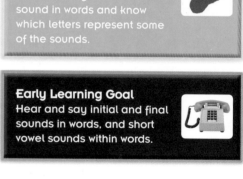

Stepping Stone
Hear and say the initial sound in words and know which letters represent some of the sounds.

Early Learning Goal
Hear and say initial and final sounds in words, and short vowel sounds within words.

© Victoria Farrow

Multicoloured mermaid

What you need
Display board; blue backing paper; shiny paper in different colours; green Cellophane; scallop shells; thin white paper; wax crayons; paint; paintbrushes; pale pink and gold or yellow paper; PVA glue; small paper plates; roll of wallpaper; scissors; felt-tipped pens; gold glitter; sticky white dots; Blu-Tack.

What to do

Involve the children in helping you to make a colourful display of a mermaid. Cover the display board with blue paper and add the title 'Our multicoloured mermaid' cut from letters in a contrasting colour. Draw the shape of the mermaid, without hair, on to a roll of wallpaper and cut it out. Cut out about 25 circles with a diameter of approximately 5cm from multicoloured shiny paper.

Place the paper mermaid on a table and ask a small group of children to help you make her tail. Cut a circle in half to make the ends of the tail, then start building up the tail with one circle, then a row of two, then three and so on, overlapping the rows.

Put the top half of the mermaid on top of a piece of pale pink paper. Draw around her upper half, then cut out and stick the pink paper on top of the outline to make her skin. Carefully draw on a face with felt-tipped pens. Place her head on top of a sheet of gold or yellow paper and draw her hair in long spiralling curls. Cut these out and invite the children to add some gold glitter for extra sparkle. Stick the mermaid on to the display board.

Cut approximately 100 circles with a diameter of 3cm from sheets of different coloured shiny paper. Prepare a fish for each child by cutting a triangle shape from the paper plates (see the activity 'Fancy fish' on page 62). Give each child a paper-plate fish shape and 20 coloured circles. Show them how to arrange and stick down the circles in overlapping rows. Add an eye made from a sticky dot with a black pupil drawn on.

©Victoria Farrow

Attach the fish to the display with Blu-Tack. Make a few scallop shells to position around the base of the display: place a sheet of thin paper over a shell and make a rubbing with a wax crayon, then add a thin wash of coloured paint in a contrasting colour. Place one of the shells in the mermaid's hand.

To finish off the display add strips of green Cellophane seaweed twisting up from the bottom.

Using the display

◆ Set up the display table with mermaid toys and other items to make a magical collection. Use the display to develop storytelling and imaginative role-play ideas.
◆ Encourage the children to think of other characters from fairy-tales and legends that could become friends with the mermaid.

Jolly pirates

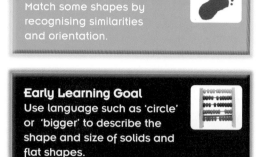

What you need
Display board; blue backing paper; off-white sugar paper; red, blue, green and black paint; brushes; brown craft paper and scraps of paper in other colours; glue; labels.

What to do

Begin by making the background to the display. Back the board with blue paper and cut out a pirate ship shape from brown paper. Cut circles from red and yellow paper for the cannon holes and cut a flag, mast and sails from black and white paper. Cut out enough rectangles and circles from off-white sugar paper for each child to make a pirate, plus extra semi-circles for headscarves.

Sit the children around a table and tell them that you would like their help to make a pirate display. Show them the pirate ship shape and ask them to make some pirates to go on board. Suggest that they take a large paper rectangle for the body and stick on smaller rectangles for the arms and legs. Add a large circle for the head with a semi-circle for the headscarf and smaller circles for the hands. Turn the pirates over and paint stripes in red, blue or green for the shirts and spots in a different colour for the headscarf. Draw in the pirates' faces, perhaps adding bristly beards or maybe an eyepatch.

Assemble ten of the pirates in and around the boat. Cut the lettering 'Ten jolly pirates' from green paper and stick it to the ship. Make bold labels for the different parts of the display, such as mast, ship, sea, flag and pirates for the children to read.

Using the display

♦ Put a treasure chest on the table in front of the display, open to reveal 'treasure', such as crowns and pasta necklaces made by the children. Add books about pirates, toy pirate ships and paper hats, maps and telescopes. Discuss the shapes and patterns that have been used and those in the crowns and necklaces.

Use the display to inspire storytelling. Make up a story about the pirates on board the ship, using language that will develop the children's understanding of positional language. For example, 'The pirates climbed on to the ship which was floating on the water. They pulled up the anchor and set sail. One of the pirates climbed to the top of the mast and looked through his telescope in search of other ships far away in the distance.'

© Victoria Farrow

Seaside frieze

What you need
Display board; stapler (adult use); roll of sugar paper; wallpaper or thick coloured paper; border in contrasting colour; paints; sponge rollers; thin paintbrushes; pencils; scissors.

What to do

Ask the children to help you create a special seaside counting frieze. Spread a roll of sugar paper over a painting table and provide the children with sponge rollers and plates of light and dark blue paint. Draw a wavy line down the centre of the paper and ask the children to help you paint the sea. Ask them to take turns using the rollers, painting dark blue one side of the line and light blue on the other. When dry, staple the paper to the display board and edge with a border roll in a contrasting colour.

Invite the children to suggest a variety of sea creatures that they would like to see on the display. You will need to think of ten different sea creatures or plants, such as a crab, seahorse, sea anemone, fish, shell, turtle, stingray, shark, starfish and octopus. Draw and cut out the objects from wallpaper or thick coloured paper so that you have, for example, one crab, two sea horses and so on up to ten.

Ask the children to sort the shapes into piles and count how many there are of each one. Invite the children to choose a shape and to decorate it in their own choice of colours and patterns. Once dry, arrange the shapes in sets on the board and label with the appropriate number. Cut out large numerals from 1 to 10 and mount them across the top of the display.

Using the display

♦ Use the display to encourage counting and number recognition. Ask the children to point out individual numerals or to tell you how many of any one creature they can see.
♦ Make sets of items and ask the children to find plastic numerals to match. Alternatively put out a numeral and ask them to count out that many shells or fish.
♦ Use gummed shapes or a printing set to count and label pictures and numerals.

Rhymes

Sitting in the sand at the seaside

We are sitting in the sand at the seaside *(sit down)*
Watching the seagulls fly, *(move arms up and down)*
Sifting the sand with our fingers *(mime sifting sand with fingers)*
And looking at a bright blue sky. *(lean back and look up)*

We are making a castle at the seaside *(mime digging and shaping a sand-castle)*
Digging the sand with a spade,
Sorting the stones from the sea shells *(kneel, and mime sorting)*
And hoping to see a mermaid. *(place hand above eyes and look around searchingly)*

We are paddling in the sea at the seaside *(mime paddling)*
Splashing in the waves and the spray, *(make splashing movements)*
Searching the seabed for a starfish *(look searchingly around the floor)*
And waving to a ship in the bay. *(wave towards the distance)*

Brenda Williams

Donkey rides

Clip, clop, donkeys trot
Up the hill and over the top.

Clip, clop, clip, clop,
On to the sands before they stop.

Ride, ride, on a donkey ride
Up the beach then along the tide.

Ride, ride, ride, ride,
Children ride at the bright seaside.

Clip, clop, clip, clop,
Back to the fields the donkeys trot.

Brenda Williams

How many fishes?

Here are the fishes swimming in the sea
How many fishes can you see?
Is it one fish, is it three?
Is it more fish you can see?
Let us count them carefully... 1 2 3 4 *(and so on, counting fish out)*

Here is a number sitting in the sea
What is the number you can see?
Is it one or is it three?
What is the number you can see? *(say number)*
Count in fishes carefully...1 2 3 4 *(and so on, counting fish in)*

Place up to ten fish in the pool for the first verse.
Place a number card up to ten, for the second verse.

Brenda Williams

Five coloured boats

Five coloured boats near a stormy shore
One tipped up, and then there were four.

Four coloured boats in a storm at sea
One tipped up, and then there were three.

Three coloured boats with all their crew
One tipped up, and then there were two.

Two coloured boats on a stormy run
One tipped up, and then there was one.

One coloured boat when the other had gone
Tipped right up, and then there were none.

Five coloured boats turned upside-down
Had to wait till the storm died down.
When the sun came out to shine
Five coloured boats sailed back in line.

Brenda Williams

Foundation Themes
The Seaside

A mermaid sings

In a deep blue sea on a rocky stone
A mermaid sings as she sits alone
And as she sings, she combs her hair
Her beautiful, golden, long, long hair.

In a deep blue sea on a rocky stone
A mermaid sings as she sits alone
And as she sings, she swings her tail
Her beautiful, silver, fish-like tail.

In a deep blue sea on a rocky stone
A mermaid sings as she sits alone
And as she sings she kisses a shell
A beautiful, pearly, deep-sea shell.

Brenda Williams

Invite the children to role-play the actions, and suggest other things the mermaid might do, such as:

… 'flashes her eyes, Her beautiful, sparkling, sea-green eyes.'

… 'waves her hand, Her beautiful, graceful, mermaid's hand.'

… 'holds a mirror, A beautiful, shiny shell-pink mirror.'

I'm going to the seaside!

I'm going to the seaside
I'm going to the sea!
These are the things
To take with me.

Sun-hat, suncream
Big floppy hat.
Stripy beach bag
For this and that.

Swimsuit, flip-flops
For me to wade.
Beach towel, T-shirt,
Bucket and spade!

Brenda Williams

Songs

Grab your hat

(Tune: Half a Pound of Tuppenny Rice)

Grab your hat, your bucket and spade,
We're going to the seaside.
While we're there we'll go to the fair, and
Whizz down the slide.

There are lovely things to eat, like
Candyfloss and ice-cream.
The sun is hot so please take care and
Slap on the suncream.

Sanchia Sewell

My bucket is full

(Tune: The Wheels on the Bus)

My bucket is full of (things I found),
Things I found, things I found, things I found.
My bucket is full of things I found,
On the beach.

The first thing I found was (lots of sand),
Lots of sand, lots of sand, lots of sand.
The first thing I found was lots of sand,
On the beach.

The second thing… pebbles small.
The third thing… pretty shells.
The fourth thing… slimy seaweed.
The fifth thing… foamy water.

Sanchia Sewell

Your footprints

(Tune: Pussycat, Pussycat, Where Have You Been?)

Look at your footprints and what can you see?
The shape of your feet is as clear as can be.
How many toes do you think you have then?
One, two, three, four, five, six, seven,
Eight, nine, ten.

Sanchia Sewell

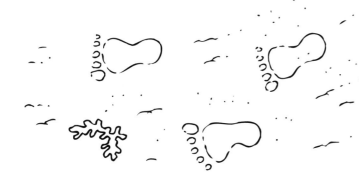

Here are some boats

(Tune: Here We Go Round the Mulberry Bush)

Here are some boats upon the sea,
Floating gently as can be. *(rock from side to side)*
Up in the sky, the clouds are dark, *(look up)*
A storm is going to start. *(nod head)*

Here are the waves that crash overboard, *(big clap)*
Here is the rain that wets us all. *(rain movements with fingers)*
Here is the wind that blows so strong, *(blow through hands)*
We hope the storm won't last long. *(hold thumbs)*

Here is the sun that peeps through the clouds, *(peep through fingers)*
Stills the wind, says, 'Not so loud'. *(finger on lips)*
Here is the rainbow glittery, *(make arc shape with arm)*
Shining over the sea.

Sanchia Sewell

Swimming fish

(Tune: This Old Man)

All the fish, in the sea,
Find that swimming is easy.
'Cause their tailfins help to move them along,
Push them forwards, very strong.

All the fish, in the sea,
Find that swimming is easy.
They have special fins to keep them straight and tall,
All fish have them big or small.

All the fish, in the sea,
Find that swimming is easy.
They have shiny scales to help them swim with ease,
Glide as smoothly as they please.

Sanchia Sewell

On a sunny day

(Tune: Sing a Song of Sixpence)

Going to the seaside on a sunny day.
Have to take the car, 'cause the sea is far away.
We've packed a lovely picnic, with lots of things to eat,
Packed towels and bathing costumes and some sandals for our feet.

Splashing in the water, playing in the sand.
Tummies feeling hungry, a picnic would be grand.
We've sandwiches and apples, peeled and sliced up thin,
And when we're finished we put all our papers in the bin.

When the day is over, and it's time to go,
We walk back to the car, our tired legs are slow.
We've packed up everything and at last we're on our way,
We say, 'Thank you' to everyone for such a lovely day.

Sanchia Sewell

Seaside shapes

Seaside sounds

Words and pictures

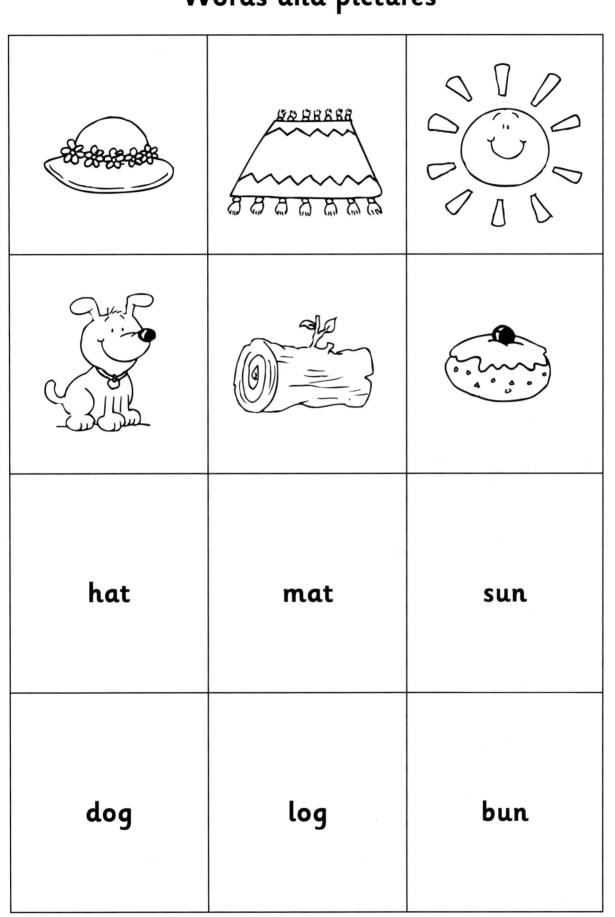

hat	mat	sun
dog	log	bun

Whose footprint?

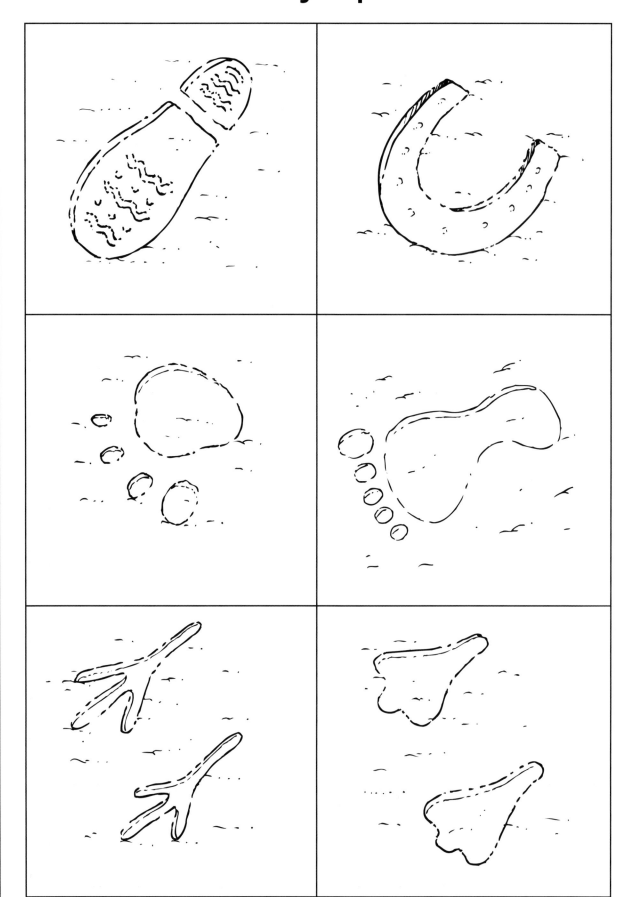

Wet or dry?

wet	dry

wet	dry

wet	dry

wet	dry

wet	dry

wet	dry

Stormy seas

Foundation Themes
The Seaside

Fishy fun

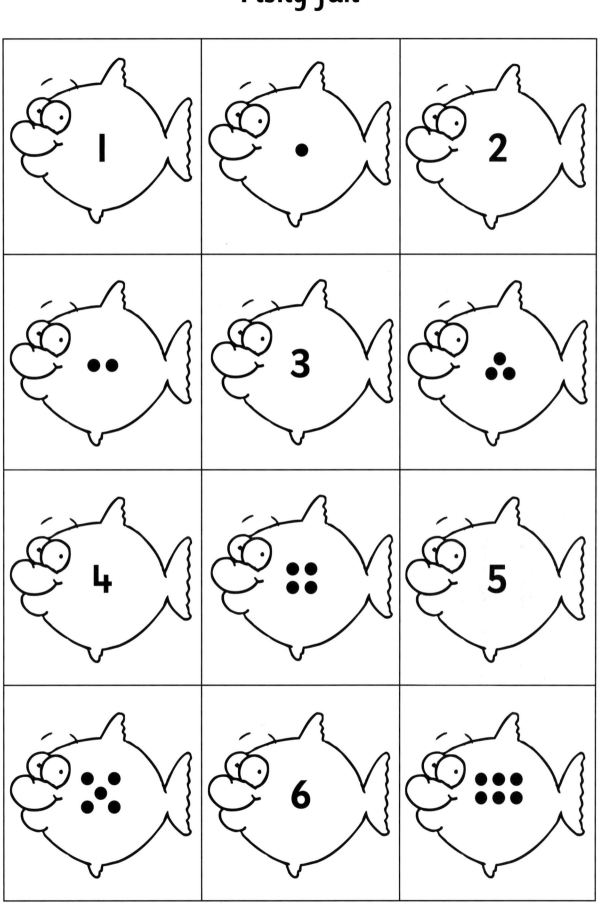

Fish patterns

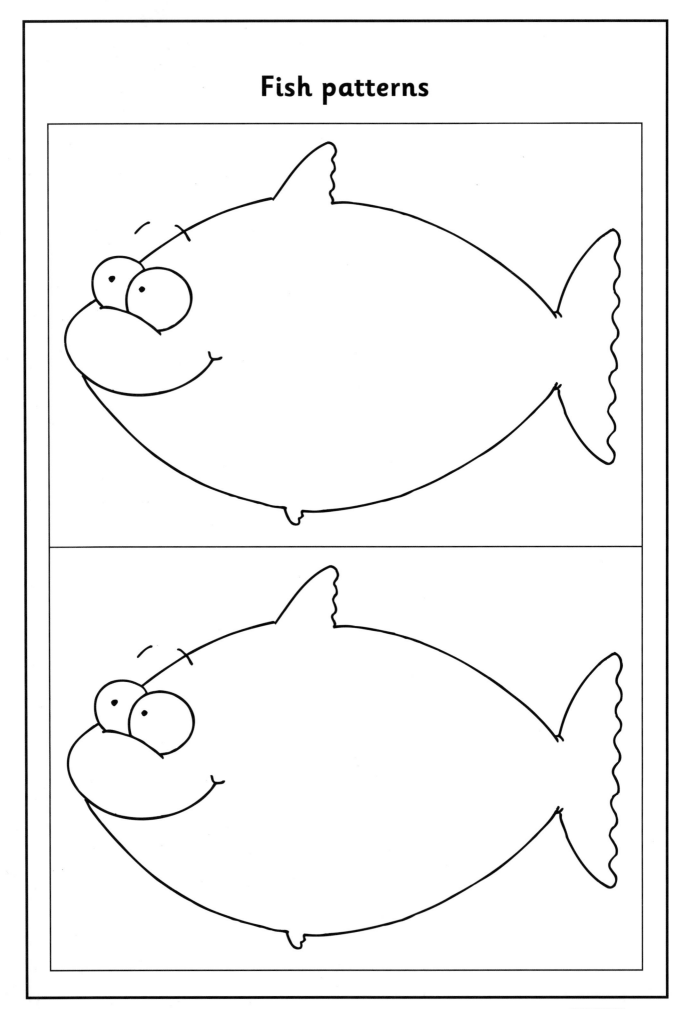

Foundation Themes

The Seaside